PREVENTING
NUCLEAR
W A R

PREVENTING NUCLEAR WAR

A Realistic Approach

Edited by

Barry M. Blechman

Indiana University Press
BLOOMINGTON

© 1985 by the Center for Strategic and International Studies,
Georgetown University

Manufactured in the United States of America

Library of Congress Cataloging in Publication Data
Main entry under title:

Preventing nuclear war.

   "Published in association with the Center for
Strategic and International Studies, Georgetown University,
Washington, D.C."
   1. Nuclear crisis control—Addresses, essays,
lectures. I. Blechman, Barry M. II. Georgetown University.
Center for Strategic and International Studies.
JX1974.8.P74   1985   327.1'7   84-43115
ISBN 0-253-34601-0
ISBN 0-253-20350-3

1   2   3   4   5   89 88 87 86 85

CONTENTS

FOREWORD

The papers included in this volume were prepared for the Nunn-Warner Working Group on Nuclear Risk Reduction and are offered solely as illustrations of the many pragmatic steps which could be implemented to help reduce the risk of nuclear war. The ideas contained in these articles should be attributed solely to their respective authors. With the exception of the report endorsing the concept of Nuclear Risk Reduction Centers, the inclusion of an article in this volume does not necessarily imply endorsement of its conclusions by the members of the Nunn-Warner Working Group on Nuclear Risk Reduction or the Georgetown Center for Strategic and International Studies.

Support for the Nunn-Warner Working Group on Nuclear Risk Reduction was provided initially by the Roosevelt Center for American Policy Studies, then under the direction of Douglas Bennet. During 1984, support for the project was provided by the Carnegie Corporation of New York. We are grateful to both institutions for their assistance.

The Center for Strategic and International Studies of Georgetown University is a research institution founded in 1962 to foster scholarship and public awareness of emerging international issues on a broad, interdisciplinary basis. It is nonpartisan and nonprofit. Its areas of research are selected in consultation with its governing bodies, and its work is entirely nonclassified.

AMOS A. JORDAN, President
Spring 1985

PREVENTING
NUCLEAR
W A R

I | A PRACTICAL APPROACH TO CONTAINING NUCLEAR DANGERS

Senator Sam Nunn and Senator John Warner

The fundamental and overriding reason for attempting to negotiate arms control arrangements is to reduce the danger of military conflict between the two great powers, particularly a conflict that involved an exchange of nuclear weapons. Although it might prove feasible in such an eventuality to limit damage to moderate levels, the danger that any use of nuclear weapons would escalate to an exchange of catastrophic proportions is substantial enough that efforts to reduce the likelihood of such a contingency deserve a high priority. The risk of war between the great powers appears to be low at present; even so, the stakes potentially at risk are sufficiently grave to merit substantial efforts to bring about even marginal reductions in whatever dangers exist.

With few exceptions, attention to arms control negotiations in recent years has tended to focus on ways to reduce the size or to alter the characteristics of U.S. and Soviet nuclear arsenals. Increasing stocks of nuclear weapons are presumed to increase the risk of nuclear war by introducing uncertainties and instabilities in the balance of power between the United States and the USSR. Similarly, weapons with certain characteristics — particularly those which could be used to destroy the strategic forces of the other side — are believed to increase the risk of nuclear attack because of their effect on the incentives each side would perceive to initiate an exchange in the event of a crisis. Thus, arms control negotiators have concentrated on attempting to bring about "deep cuts" in strategic arsenals, and also to eliminate preferentially those weapons believed to make the strategic balance less stable.

1

In short, nuclear arms control negotiations have been attempting primarily to reduce the risk of nuclear war indirectly. They have been concentrating on the "capabilities" of the two sides to wage nuclear war. These efforts obviously are important and should be continued. But there is also the matter of "intentions." In addition to having certain capabilities, a nation needs a reason to wage war — either a malevolent intention of its own or a perception that an opponent has such an intention and therefore it would be prudent to strike first.

Negotiations can do little about malevolent intentions. In these cases it is essential to maintain powerful military forces capable of making clear to a potential aggressor that the cost of initiating conflict would be far greater than any potential gain. Negotiations, however, can help to reduce the possibility of erroneous perceptions of the other side's intentions — to facilitate communications between the two nations in crises and to build confidence in both states that the other does not intend to initiate conflict. Even if one side does have malevolent intentions, negotiated measures of confidence-building and communications can strengthen deterrence by reducing the danger of war by accident or inadvertence. Nuclear confidence-building measures can serve the additional function, in the event of a war between the two great powers, of assuring each nation that the conflict could be maintained on the conventional level and not escalate to the use of nuclear weapons.

One of the benefits of this approach to nuclear arms control is that it typically involves relatively small and noncontroversial steps, often technical arrangements that can be put in place without being complicated by the sharp political and ideological differences between the United States and the USSR. (Joseph S. Nye, Jr., places this approach to arms control in the broader perspective of U.S.-Soviet relations in Chapter 2.) Indeed, the two nations already have reached several agreements that can be considered part of this general approach to reducing the risk of nuclear war. William J. Lynn outlines these precedents in Chapter 3 of this volume, and the text of several other agreements are reproduced as appendixes. But there are many other things that could be done — pragmatic, politically feasible means of reducing the danger of the use of nuclear weapons.

Since 1982, we have cochaired a working group established to develop, evaluate, and — when appropriate — promote specific, pragmatic, and politically feasible means of making the use of nuclear weapons less likely. In addition to ourselves, the working group included James Schlesinger, the former Secretary of Defense; Brent Scowcroft, President Ford's

National Security Advisor; Richard Ellis, United States Commissioner on the U.S.-USSR Standing Consultative Commission; Bobby Inman, formerly Deputy Director of Central Intelligence; William Hyland, formerly Deputy National Security Advisor (who served as the group's secretary); William Perry, formerly Under Secretary of Defense for Research and Engineering; Don Rice, President of the RAND Corporation; and Barry Blechman, a senior fellow at the Center for Strategic and International Studies. The Nunn-Warner Working Group on Nuclear Risk Reduction was established to explore pragmatic means of making the use of nuclear weapons less likely — means of improving communications and understanding between the United States and the USSR and measures to help build confidence between the two great powers that neither intends to initiate a nuclear conflict.

The group has met periodically over the past two years to consider a variety of ideas and proposals. In November 1983, it issued an interim report recommending that the United States and the USSR consider establishing "Nuclear Risk Reduction Centers" in their respective capitals to carry out a variety of functions that would contribute to a reduced danger of nuclear conflict. These centers would maintain a twenty-four-hour watch on situations that could lead to nuclear confrontations. They would be linked by sophisticated, real-time communications channels and might also include liaison officers from the second nation among their staffs. In addition to their roles during and prior to crises, they could serve as the forum for a variety of negotiations and information exchanges during normal times — all intended to control nuclear risks. The text of the Nunn-Warner report on Nuclear Risk Reduction Centers is included as Appendix A. The idea is discussed at greater length in an article by Richard K. Betts, Chapter 5 of this volume.

A wide range of measures that might also be considered for U.S.-Soviet negotiations could help to reduce the risk of nuclear war.

For one, it would be possible to enhance the physical means of communicating between the two nations in the event of a nuclear crisis. The United States and the USSR agreed to install a dedicated communications link for the use of the two heads-of-state in the wake of the Cuban Missile Crisis. The "Hot Line" Agreement was completed in 1963 and improved in 1971 when a satellite communications system was added to the existing land lines. In 1984, the hot line was improved again when the United States and the USSR agreed to add a facsimile transmission link to the existing teletype system. Additional measures are possible. President

Reagan, for example, has proposed that an additional communications channel be established between the U.S. Department of Defense and the Soviet Defense Ministry for the exchange of technical information in the event of a crisis. He also has proposed that the two sides agree to upgrade the communications links between their respective capitals and their embassies in Moscow and Washington. (The text of the Defense Department study that recommended these measures is included in Appendix C.)

Second, the United States and the Soviet Union could exchange much more information about their respective nuclear forces and doctrines, with a view toward clarifying ambiguities, reducing suspicions, and building confidence of nonhostile intent. The two sides, for example, could maintain a common data base describing their strategic forces. Such a data base was created for the SALT II Treaty; it would be a relatively easy matter to update it periodically and to expand it to include forces not now counted.

The two great powers might also agree to notify each other prior to tests of strategic missiles and aircraft. The SALT II Treaty includes a requirement that certain types of tests be announced in advance. The United States has proposed to expand these requirements in the START negotiations; the Soviet Union has made somewhat related proposals.

Thought might also be given to instituting periodic meetings between military representatives of the two great powers. As explained by Wade J. Williams in Chapter 9, such a dialogue could help to improve mutual understanding and reduce suspicions on the two sides. In these periodic meetings, or in other forums, it might be helpful if each side informed the other of the types of strategic operations, tests, or development programs that caused concern. Such talks need not lead to any sort of formal agreement (and probably would not), but they could lead each side to eliminate practices which the other found needlessly provocative. For example, the USSR sometimes launches several missiles at one time in military exercises. This causes some concern when detected by U.S. warning systems. Similarly, the Soviets have complained about certain U.S. exercises involving strategic bombers. A frank exchange of views on these subjects might lead to unilateral actions to avoid certain practices.

For that matter, it might be possible to negotiate formal, mutual restraints in certain strategic operations or tests of certain types of strategic weapons. Obviously, any such proposal would have to be examined carefully on its merits; there would be risks as well as benefits in virtually any such proposal. Still, the idea bears exploration. Alan J. Vick and James A. Thomson explore limits on strategic operations in Chapter 7.

Sidney D. Drell and Theodore J. Ralston analyze the potential utility of limitations on certain weapon tests in Chapter 6.

Third, the United States and the USSR might agree on joint planning for certain contingencies involving nuclear threats by third parties. Despite their very real differences, the two great powers do have certain interests in common — controlling the risk of nuclear terrorism being one of them. In the years ahead, nuclear weapon capabilities will almost certainly spread to additional nations. The risk that a weapon might fall into the hands of a subnational group or rogue national leader may be small, but it will almost certainly rise over the years. It would be prudent for U.S. and Soviet representatives to discuss how the two nations might behave in various contingencies; to think through possible crises and map out potential forms of cooperation. For example, what if there were an unexplained nuclear explosion somewhere? How would the two sides react? Or say there was a threat from a terrorist group to detonate a weapon if certain demands were not met? Or what if a nuclear weapon or the fissile material for one or more weapons were discovered to be missing? Or what if an intelligence agency determined that a subnational organization was on the verge of acquiring a nuclear capability? Joint planning for these types of contingencies — simply talking through the types of actions which would and would not be helpful — could well facilitate effective cooperation should the threat ever become real. Barry M. Blechman discusses the possible use of Nuclear Risk Reduction Centers to control the danger of nuclear terrorism in Chapter 4.

Finally, the United States and the USSR could agree to certain physical measures to help reduce the risk of accidental or inadvertent nuclear war. Victor A. Utgoff describes one such idea in Chapter 8 of this volume. He analyzes the costs and benefits of an agreement by the United States and the USSR to install unmanned, tamper-proof radars at each other's missile fields. These radars would detect the launch of a missile with an extremely high probability and send an encrypted signal back to the other nation. Different, and also encrypted, signals would also be sent at other times to ensure that the system was working properly. The installation of such a system would complement each side's early warning satellites, helping to avoid unnecessary — and possibly provocative — reactions to false warnings of attack and building confidence that neither side would attempt a surprise attack. As Utgoff points out, these types of unmanned, remote-sensor systems might have other applications as well in helping to reduce the risk of nuclear war.

In short, there are many potential practical steps to reduce the dangers implied by the existence of nuclear weapons. Each such measure requires careful and objective evaluation; none are without some costs and risks. Still, these ideas are worth exploring. We commend them to the attention of citizens and officials.

2 | Nuclear Risk Reduction Measures and U.S.–Soviet Relations

Joseph S. Nye, Jr.

SINCE THE DECLINE of détente in the 1970s, there has been an increase in public concern about U.S.-Soviet relations and the risk of nuclear war. This is not the first time that public concern has been aroused, nor is it likely to be the last time. Managing relations with the USSR has never been easy for the United States.

One reason is the Soviet Union. The marriage of the Russian empire and a universalistic ideology has produced a state which sometimes looks like a traditional great power and sometimes like an expansionist revolutionary power. A repressive and secretive political system frustrates efforts to fathom Soviet intentions. It is small wonder that Americans have often divided views about the nature of their principal opponent. Even lifelong experts do not agree about the nature of the Soviet state and its goals. Although the Soviet Union will remain an enigma, its nuclear capability remains an inescapable fact, and there is broad public concern over whether we can manage the relationship in a manner that reduces the risk of nuclear war.

U.S.–SOVIET RELATIONS AND NUCLEAR RISKS

There are several deep-seated reasons to believe that tension is likely to be a continual feature in U.S.–Soviet relations. First, as Tocqueville already saw in the nineteenth century, the enormous size and resources of the Russian and American nations foreshadowed a future bipolar

7

rivalry. Then in 1917, the Bolshevik Revolution added a layer of deep ideological incompatibility. When the second World War destroyed the multination balance of power existing before 1939, it left a bipolar structure of world power centered on the U.S.–Soviet rivalry. The accumulation of vast nuclear arsenals overshadowing those of all other nations has consolidated that "special relationship." From a power politics point of view, the probability of tension is built into the very structure of the relationship.

Nonetheless, at different times, there have been different degrees of tensions and hostility. American attitudes, responding in part to Soviet tactical moves and in part to the requirements of democratic politics, have tended to alternate between overemphasis and underemphasis on the threatening nature of Soviet objectives. The result has been an inconsistency in policy and missed opportunities. During the Cold War, our exaggeration of Soviet capabilities prevented us from negotiating at a time when our position was strong. Subsequently, the ideological interpretation of policy and domestic political constraints prevented American policy from exploiting the diplomatic opportunities in the Sino-Soviet split for more than a decade after it occurred in the late 1950s. Conversely, the enthusiasm for détente in the 1960s and early 1970s led American officials to underestimate the Soviet military buildup, delay an appropriate response, and encourage false domestic expectations of future restraint in Soviet international behavior.

At the same time, it is worth remembering that the worst outcome has not occurred. Despite hostility, there has also been prudence in managing the world's first nuclear balance of power. The destructiveness of nuclear weapons introduced a disproportion between most ends that the superpowers seek and the major military means at their disposal.

This situation has led to the evolution by a process of trial and error of some primitive rules for avoiding and managing crises. The rules are so primitive that they might more correctly be called prudent practices. Indeed, they began well before the onset of détente. As described by Stanley Hoffmann, "one such informal rule was the non-resort to atomic weapons . . . . A second rule was the avoidance of direct military clashes between the armed forces. This meant that their games of chicken had to end with the retreat of one of the players rather than with a fight . . . . A third element was the slow (and for America) painful learning of limited wars . . . calculated so as to limit the risks of escalation, even if those constraints made a clearcut victory or a rapid settlement impossible. Later came the beginnings of nuclear arms control between Washington and Moscow."[1] Rudimentary as these rules or prudent practices are, they are significant if one believes that a stable balance of power requires a degree of moderation in the actors' behavior, as well as military balance.

Where there is a degree of common interest in stability, the balance of power can become a positive game in which both sides win. Indeed, an international "regime"—a set of tacit or explicit rules and procedures—may be developed to encourage a stabilizing perspective of long-range rather than short-range self-interest. The nineteenth-century balance of power and the contrast between Bismarck's restraint and the failure of his successors is often cited as an example.

To say that the postwar U.S.–Soviet balance of power has been embedded in such a regime would be to stretch the point.[2] The rules are ambiguous and not openly accepted by both sides. In 1972 and 1973, Nixon and Brezhnev signed agreements that seemed to codify the rules, but the ambiguities (such as exceptions for "wars of national liberation") later led to a sense of cheating and deception after the Middle East War of 1973 and the Soviet transport of Cuban troops to Angola in 1975 and 1976. Moreover, an agreed regime implies reciprocity and flexibility in bargaining behavior as the opponents seek to avoid jeopardizing the regime. In U.S.–Soviet relations, however, reciprocity has proven to be limited in time and on issues. It is difficult to "bank goodwill" from one time or issue to another in the relationship. While both sides have a degree of interest in preserving stability in the form of preserving nuclear bipolarity and the avoidance of nuclear war, their competition makes it impossible to agree on the status quo. While a common interest exists, it is severely limited and strained by the competitive dimension.

Another reason why the effects of this common interest are limited is the difficulty of communication between the two societies. The secretive nature of Soviet society makes it something of a "black box" to us. We see what comes out of the box, but can't understand what goes on inside it. It is difficult to bring evidence to bear on our differences of opinion over Soviet intentions and the nature of their internal processes. Obviously, this situation can result in misperceptions, but it is hard to prove what is or is not a misperception. There is none of the relative transparency that characterizes relations with most countries.

This indeterminacy exacerbates the struggle for definition and control of appropriate policy responses in the United States. American foreign policy making is a notably untidy process. In the words of a great constitutional scholar, the constitution establishes an invitation to struggle for the control of foreign policy.[3] Thus, it is not surprising that we find it hard to figure out what is happening in a black box.

At the same time, incoherence and inconsistency in U.S. policy can lead to Soviet misperceptions and miscalculations of American intentions and concerns. Stalin must certainly have been surprised by Truman's reaction in 1950 so soon after the United States had declared Korea outside its defense perimeter. Khrushchev may also have been surprised by the strength of Kennedy's reaction to the emplacement of missiles in Cuba after the acceptance of defeat at the Bay of Pigs. Soviet intentions are opaque to Americans because of Soviet secrecy. U.S. intentions may be opaque to Soviet leaders because of incoherence and multiple—and often contradictory—signals. They may be a black box to us, but we may confuse them with "white noise."

In dealing with a stronger Soviet Union in an age of nuclear parity, we will not have as much leeway for incoherence, inconsistency, and inefficiency as in earlier periods. The fact that past crises have not led to nuclear war in nearly four decades cannot justify complacency about the future. Nuclear risk reduction deserves a high policy priority.

TYPES OF REDUCTION MEASURES

Efforts to reduce the risk of nuclear war must start with an understanding of the likely paths by which a nuclear war might begin. As Table 2-1 illustrates, there are at least five significantly different paths by which a nuclear war might arise: (1) escalation of conventional wars to nuclear ones, (2) preemptive attacks launched in desperation in times of crises because one side believes (rightly or wrongly) that the other intends to strike first, (3) accidental uses of nuclear weapons resulting from malfunctions of men or machines, (4) nuclear wars initiated by nuclear armed nations other than the superpowers or by terrorist organizations, and (5) surprise attacks by one superpower on all or part of the nuclear forces of the other. For each of these generic paths, a number of possible scenarios can be constructed.[4]

There are also a variety of actions that can be taken to reduce the likelihood of each path leading to nuclear war. Many of these measures

Table 2-1
Nuclear Risk Reduction

PATHS To Nuclear War (ranked by probability)	FACTORS Affecting Likelihood of Path	ACTIONS To Reduce Likelihood of Path
1. Escalation of conventional war	U.S.–Soviet conventional war Balance of general purpose forces Vulnerability of theater nuclear forces Misperception/miscalculation	Crisis prevention and management Maintain balance of general purpose forces Reduce vulnerability of theater nuclear forces Improve command/control
2. Preemption in crisis	War appears imminent and unavoidable Balance of nuclear forces Vulnerability of nuclear forces Misperception/miscalculation	Crisis prevention and management Maintain balance of nuclear forces Reduce vulnerability of nuclear forces Maintain ability to launch vulnerable forces on warning
3. Accidental or unauthorized use	Procedures and devices designed to prevent accidents and unauthorized use (e.g., Permissive Action Links) Communication systems	Improve procedures and devices Improve communication systems Crisis prevention and management
4. Initiation by a third party	Third-party access to nuclear weapons and delivery systems U.S. and Soviet presence in conflict areas	Inhibit nuclear proliferation Crisis prevention and management
5. Surprise attack	Extreme U.S.–Soviet hostility Balance of nuclear forces Vulnerability of nuclear forces Misperception/miscalculation Irrationality	Strengthen incentives for peace Maintain balance of nuclear forces Reduce vulnerability of nuclear forces Achieve arms control (e.g., comprehensive test ban)

of nuclear risk reduction involve unilateral political and military measures to enhance deterrence, reduce the vulnerability of forces, reassure other nations, and improve procedures and devices to prevent accidents or unauthorized use. In other words, many significant measures of nuclear risk reduction do not require cooperative action with the Soviet Union. At the same time, as Table 2-1 indicates, cooperative measures of crisis prevention and management can also help to reduce the risk of war associated with nearly all of the paths.

Most nuclear risk reduction measures share a common approach. In contrast to those aspects of arms control and disarmament that focus on reductions of the number of nuclear weapons, risk reduction measures are more concerned with the prospects of use of such weapons regardless of numbers. On the other hand, the terminology surrounding nuclear risk reduction measures is sometimes confusing, with terms like *crisis management, crisis prevention, stabilization,* and *confidence-building* often used in overlapping ways. Measures may vary along dimensions of technical vs. political, unilateral vs. cooperative, global vs. regional, general vs. specific, and so forth. Sometimes *confidence-building measures* is narrowly used to describe specific techni-cal or military initiatives. But the term can also be used more broadly to refer to any efforts to increase confidence and predictability.

Another way to distinguish various nuclear risk reduction measures is by their proximity in time to the causes of a possible nuclear war. (See Table 2-2.) With any complex event, we often distinguish pre-cipitating, contributory, and deep causes. For example, the assassina-tion of the Austrian Archduke and the rigidity of mobilization sched-ules were precipitating causes of World War I; the Austro-Russian competition in the Balkans and Serbian adventurism were contribu-tory or intermediate causes; and the increased rigidity in European alliances was a deep cause. Or to use the simple metaphor of starting a fire: a match is a precipitating cause; kindling is an intermediate cause; and the piling up of logs is a deep cause.

Table 5-2 differentiates risk reduction measures in these terms. *Crisis management* refers to measures to deal with a crisis once it has begun, and to prevent the precipitating factors that could lead to war. *Crisis prevention* refers to efforts to deal with intermediate or contributory causes that give rise to the crises in the first place. *Long-range stabiliza-tion* relates to efforts to deal with the basic causes of conflict inherent in the U.S.–Soviet relationship. All three levels are part of nuclear risk

Table 2-2

Approach to U.S.–Soviet Nuclear Risk Reductions

	Basic Goals	General Strategies	Some CBMs and Stabilization Measures
1. Crisis management (of possible precipitating causes of nuclear war)	Crisis stability Credibility Limits Termination	SOPs that buy time Clear signals Constant communication Civilian control of force movements Termination plans	Declaratory policy Crisis exercises Hot line Crisis center
2. Crisis prevention (of possible contributory causes of nuclear crises)	Avoid misperception and miscalculation of interests Avoid loss of control to small states Avoid loss of control due to military mistakes	Preventive diplomacy Classic diplomacy Early consultations General and specific limits	Mediation Military zones, buffers, etc. Regular meetings Arms transfer talks Nonproliferation
3. Long-Run stabilization (of basic conflict that creates risks of nuclear crises and war)	Increase transparency and predictability Demonstrate common interest	Increase contacts Increase reciprocity	Arms control Monitoring/inspection TAC talks Exchanges

reduction. At each level, confidence-building measures and stabiliza-tion devices can be designed to increase openness and predictability, provide warning and reassurance, and demonstrate a common inter-est. In this broad sense, such measures can touch the core as well as the marginal dimensions of conflict.[5] We can look at the costs, benefits, and limits of such measures at each level.

CRISIS MANAGEMENT MEASURES

The United States and the Soviet Union have been involved in the practice of crisis management for a long time, at least since the Berlin Crisis of 1948. In Berlin (then and later), Korea, Cuba, Vietnam, and the Middle East, the two superpowers established limits on their objectives and means which successfully avoided the escalation of such crises to U.S.–Soviet war (not to mention nuclear war). As mentioned earlier, however, such crisis management tended to be ad hoc prudent practices, rather than codified rules or procedures.

Alexander George lists seven operational requirements for crisis management:[6]

1. Each side must maintain top-level civilian control over military options.
2. The tempo of military movements may have to be slowed to provide time for diplomatic exchanges.
3. Military movements must be coordinated into diplomatic strategy, including a strategy for termination.
4. Military signals of resolve must be consistent with limited diplo-matic objectives.
5. Moves that give the impression of resort to large-scale warfare and give an incentive for preemption should be avoided.
6. Options should be chosen that signal a way out of the crisis other than a military solution.
7. Proposals should be formulated that are compatible with the opponent's fundamental interests.

Some of the requirements are basically prudent practice that can be applied unilaterally; for example, standard operating procedures (SOPs) that ensure civilian control and integration of military and diplomatic moves in single strategy. Crisis control exercises and political-military games can help to develop such SOPs. Another useful device are SOPs that buy time. One suggestion is a declaratory policy of "no second strike in response to small scale nuclear attacks until there has been communication with the enemy."[7] In principle, both sides could agree to make such a statement.

Rapid and reliable communication is an essential component of crisis management. Recognition of the importance of communication gave rise to one of the first formal cooperative crisis management procedures, the hot line established in the aftermath of the Cuban Missile Crisis. While its existence is a useful safety device, in practice the hot line has rarely been used, and has not really been a substitute for more formal diplomatic communications. Various proposals have been made to upgrade the hot line to a visual and voice link or to supplement it by establishing a permanently manned crisis control center. The visual/voice link, however, does not guarantee better communication and control in a crisis. On the contrary, it may communicate (rightly or wrongly) *too much* information (such as strain or fatigue), while making careful formulation of a response more difficult. In 1984, the United States and the Soviet Union agreed to a modest upgrading of the hot line by adding the capability to transmit facsimiles.[8]

Another idea that has recently received a good deal of attention is the proposal by Senators Nunn and Warner that the United States and the USSR establish crisis control centers.[9] The value of the centers would vary with the crisis path or scenario that is assumed. They might be particularly valuable in case of accidental or catalytic uses of a nuclear device (paths 3 and 4 in Table 2-1) when not only rapid communication would be important, but rapid agreement among experts on the nature of technical evidence might be necessary to avoid misperception or overreaction. They might be less valuable in cases of preemption or deliberate escalation or bluff in a conventional war situation (paths 1 and 2 in Table 2-1). While permanent staffs might have developed ways to calibrate each other's reliability, it is not clear that they would be at a high enough level to be fully informed of their government's actions in such situations. In that case, the centers might be ignored or, even worse, the trust or calibration at the staff level might be turned to deceptive purposes by higher-level decision-makers.

In short, crisis management measures for nuclear risk reduction will involve a major component of unilateral domestic procedures. Some elements of such procedures might be discussed with the Soviets. Both declaratory policy on standard procedures for response to small (possibly accidental) attacks and general discussion of procedures for avoiding accidental and unauthorized use might be explored. Similarly, existing centers might provide expertise that would reinforce rapid communication in cases of accidental or third-party use. But in regard to other paths toward war in a crisis, most of the requirements for crisis management listed by Alexander George will have to be met by improved domestic procedures, good communication, and ad hoc limits established in particular crisis bargaining situations. Or to put the point in a slightly different way, there is a greater margin for nuclear risk reduction in preventing, rather than managing, crises.

CRISIS PREVENTION

Crises can arise from a variety of sources. One way is through U.S. or Soviet misperception or miscalculation of the other side's interests and likely responses. Berlin, Korea, and Cuba are cases in point. Such crises may be averted by effective deterrence when relative stakes and capabilities are clear to both sides, but many ambiguous cases exist — the Persian Gulf, for example, which is in the Soviet Union's geographical "back yard" but in the Western world's economic "front yard."

Another source of crisis lies in the political instability of Third World states. With more than one hundred fragile polities suffering the pressures of turbulent social change, there is almost always bound to be some government or its opponents who will "search for borrowed power" by involving the United States or the Soviet Union in local conflicts.[10] Among the ways to avert small states' conflicts becoming East-West crises are preventive diplomacy and cooperative diplomatic measures with the Soviet Union.

Yet a third source of serious crisis could arise in situations where U.S. and Soviet forces confront each other. In Europe, the full military panoply of the NATO and Warsaw Pact alliances face each other. In such circumstances, there is always some danger of military accident, mistake, or miscalculation. A number of military confidence-building and disengagement measures have been suggested to prevent such a possible crisis.

Military CBMs can be a limited but useful form of crisis prevention. The Agreement on Incidents at Sea, with its procedures for early and regular consultation, has helped to defuse what was once a series of minor but aggravating incidents. At the strategic level, the SALT treaties provide for noninterference with national technical means of verification, and the existence of the SCC provides a channel to raise questions regarding possible violation of the SALT agreements. One could envisage further measures such as prior notification of missile launches or agreements to establish submarine standoff zones which might avert crises through military accidents or misperceptions. Similarly, at the regional level in Europe, notification of military maneuvers, drawbacks of armored divisions, removal of bridging equipment, and rights to observe military movements above a certain size are among the useful confidence-building measures that are likely to be discussed in the Stockholm Conference on Disarmament in Europe.

If one regards the prospects of crisis by accident or military mistake to be relatively low in the first place, however, these measures are of limited importance. And skeptics warn that there are potential costs attached to some CBMs. False confidence may be as great a danger as unwarranted suspicion. Indeed, the popularity of CBMs in Europe may reflect a political tendency to substitute them for the last détente of the seventies. Richard Betts argues, for example, that there have been no pure surprise attacks in this century; the primary problem of surprise attack is not intelligence warning, but political disbelief. If CBMs contribute to a lulling effect, they may enhance conditions for surprise. Betts favors CBMs that force the exchange of information with closed societies or enhance military warning, but is skeptical of those that would curtail NATO's preparedness.[11]

The danger of building false confidence is not a trivial problem. One way to protect against it is to divide CBMs into those with a primary military purpose and those with a primary political function. In fact, both types have political *effects,* but those with a military purpose of providing warning, information, or constraint on offensive preparations are less dangerous than those entered into *solely* to improve the political climate. At least in the former case there is some built-in protection against deception. The best approach to CBMs is to start with the militarily useful and hope for a bonus effect on the political climate rather than vice versa.

A more likely source of crisis than attack in Europe is a conflict in the Third World into which the superpowers are progressively drawn by local actors. This is the area which the general principles of 1972 and

1973 were supposed to affect, but as argued above, the generality and ambiguity of those agreements led to misunderstanding rather than cooperation in conflict prevention. Given the difficulty of achieving U.S.-Soviet cooperation in this area, the first devices to be tried should be unilateral or multilateral preventive diplomacy. This has worked in situations like the Sinai, Zaire, and Zimbabwe, but not in other cases like the West Bank, the Horn of Africa, or Namibia.

Despite the difficulty of getting precision in U.S. and Soviet interpretations of general principles, there have been a number of instances when the two states have used classic diplomatic devices of crisis prevention such as spheres of influence, neutralization, buffer states, and international forces.[12] Example are the treatment of Finland and Austria in the first postwar decade, of Laos in 1961, and of Cuba in 1962 and 1970. One could imagine enhancing such classic practices by regular or early consultations on crisis prevention regarding specific situations. One could do likewise under the rubric of discussions of conventional arms transfers or on the nonproliferation of nuclear weapons.[13]

Looking at crisis prevention measures, we find, as we did with crisis management, that there is a significant role for unilateral measures. We also note that political measures that deal with specific cases, often by classic diplomatic means, are more valuable than statements of general principles. Indeed, the latter may be counterproductive unless efforts at implementation bring a more detailed level of agreement. Military CBMs to reduce risks of accidents and mistakes can be useful within narrow limits. More basic efforts to control the security relationships have to go deeper into the nature of the overall conflict between the two countries.

LONG-RUN STABILIZATION

Stability can have several meanings in U.S.-Soviet relations. Political stability is difficult to agree upon because the two societies have different ideological perceptions of the legitimacy of the status quo over the long run. On the other hand, both sides may find common prudential interests in interim or specific situations of political stability in which long-run questions of legitimacy can be begged. Moreover, both sides may also discover joint interests in crisis stability (the absence of incentive to preempt in a crisis), and a less vigorous arms race if economic constraints continue to grow.

Given the different nature of the two societies, explicit agreement on long-run stabilization will not be easy. But given also that there is some finite probability of nuclear deterrence failing by accident or miscalculation, a strategy for nuclear risk reduction cannot ignore the possibility of trying to ameliorate the basic conditions of conflict, however slow that may be. As argued previously, the secretive nature of Soviet society and the disparate nature of our two societies enhances the dangers of miscalculation as a path to war. Thus one of the goals of long-run nuclear risk reduction measures is to increase the transparency and predictability in the U.S.–Soviet relationship as a means of reducing the chances of miscalculation. The aim is to poke holes in the black box. A second goal of such measures is the canonical CBM goal of demonstrating the existence of common interests between the two rivals. And as has been noted in relation to more restricted CBMs, care must be taken to design the measures to enhance warning and minimize chances for deception. The pursuit of such goals would involve strategies of increased contacts and exchanges, particularly those which develop in a climate of reciprocity. Openness and information on the Soviet side is a key objective. There are a variety of such exchanges and contacts; the following discussion deals with those in the military domain.

Viewed from this perspective, one of the potentially most significant CBMs and stabilization measures is the process of arms control negotiations. All too often, arms control efforts have been judged solely in terms of formal treaties and reductions in numbers of existing weapons. But arms control can also contribute to the enhancement of transparency and reciprocity in the relationship. When one compares the discussions in the 1950s with today's, it is evident that the Soviet Union has gradually come to disclose more information. Provisions such as noninterference with national technical means, regular meetings of delegations and of the SCC, acceptance of cooperative surveillance measures (such as in the Treaty on Peaceful Explosions), and provisions for exchange of information and establishment of common data bases are cases in point.

In fact, if one wished to enhance the role of arms control as a CBM or stabilization measure, one might supplement the existing negotiations by incorporating them in a broader framework of nuclear stabilization talks.[14] Such an approach would have several tracks.

Talks would deliberately be designed to enhance transparency and communication rather than to reach reductions. They might include, for example, regular meetings between the chairman of the Joint Chiefs of Staff and his Soviet counterpart. They would not necessarily seek a particular agreement but would discuss specific problems relating to stability- and confidence-building measures, such as occur in the context of current agreements for controlling naval incidents at sea. In fact, this might be a significant, if less obvious, role for a joint crisis control center. Officially, it would coordinate U.S. and Soviet reactions if a nuclear weapon were exploded by a terrorist group or a Third World country. But it might also involve the exchange of information more generally in relation to stabilization measures.

Yet another track in the nuclear-stabilization framework could consist of seeking limited agreement where possible. We have seen examples of this approach relating to physical areas: fencing off Antarctica from the arms race, for example, or fencing off the seabeds and outer space from nuclear weapons. We've also seen it in certain technologies. Whatever the merits of particular proposals — the list can be readily multiplied — the larger point is that formal arms reduction talks are only part of the repertoire of arms control when approached as a strategy for nuclear risk reduction.

Naturally, there are certain risks to approaching arms control as a CBM or stabilization measure. One danger is that public opinion in democracies would be lulled by the comforting existence of the process and would underinvest in defense. The effect of SALT in the 1970s is sometimes cited as an example. On the other hand, this lulling effect can be exaggerated. U.S. defense budgets declined in the seventies as a result of changing domestic priorities and reaction to the Vietnam War, well before SALT I, and the debate over SALT II probably accentuated attention to defense issues. In any case, overall Soviet political behavior was probably more important in its effects on U.S. opinion than the existence of arms control talks. Recent events have shown that arms control may be a domestic political necessity in democracies. If so, it can be better designed to fill its role as a nuclear risk reduction measure.

POLITICAL CLIMATE AND LINKAGE

There will always be linkage between nuclear-stabilization measures and U.S.-Soviet relations generally — but there are two types of linkage. One type is inherent: Whether we wanted to or not, our democracy could not ignore a bloody invasion of Poland or Iran. The other type is tactical, in which we choose to make an explicit connection. The latter is a question of degree and of choice. There may be a situation in which, if we had a richer menu of stabilization measures, we would be more flexible in some linkage possibilities instead of having no choice but to put pressure on the single major arms control negotiation. It is interesting to note that the Reagan Administration came into office committed to the idea of tactical linkage, but seems largely to have eschewed it in practice. In any case, the effect of a worsening climate of relations on various risk reduction measures will depend on how an administration chooses to respond in light of public perceptions of particular Soviet behavior, the reaction of allies, and the existence (or absence) of other policy instruments for response to Soviet behavior.

Generally, an improving climate will help new initiatives, and a worsening political climate will make new measures difficult to initiate. Nonetheless, if the United States is publicly perceived to be more at fault, the worsening climate may increase popular demands to enhance certain existing stabilization measures. Thus, in the area of crisis management, deteriorating relations might increase pressure to upgrade the hot line or to establish a crisis control center, but the same conditions may make it difficult to negotiate the details of a new initiative. In the domain of crisis prevention, a deteriorating climate need not interfere with ad hoc classic measures of averting crises. After all, these early forms of crisis prevention originated at the height of the Cold War as a result of the prudential concerns outlined at the beginning of this paper. On the other hand, new initiatives in consultations or military CBMs for crisis prevention would be difficult to develop in a climate of deteriorating relations. Roughly the same pattern could be expected to be true for long-range stabilization measures. Domestic concern might lead to pressures to initiate arms control talks, but mistrust would probably make their completion more difficult. At the same time, the willingness to initiate new exchanges, stabilization talks, or cooperative measures is likely to be less under deteriorating relations.

CONCLUSION

The basic conflict between the United States and the Soviet Union has deep roots and will persist for a long time. During that time, there will be some danger of a breakdown of deterrence. The paths are outlined in Table 2-1. The most likely path is through miscalculation of intentions and escalation in an area of ambiguous interests in the Third World. A somewhat less probable but still significant path to breakdown would be through accident, mistake, or chaos surrounding unforeseen events in situations where the two military forces confront each other. Further in the future, and somewhat lower in probability, is the prospect of catalytic nuclear war started by a third party. Least likely of the paths is a pure "bolt out of the blue" surprise attack.

A variety of measures can be taken to reduce the risk of nuclear war along each of these paths. Many of the confidence-building measures that stress early warning (such as notification of multiple missile launches) are aimed at the lowest probability paths. Nonetheless, if well designed, they can have some military value and a larger political symbolic value. Other measures such as improving physical communications (for example, the hot line upgrade) or sharing and evaluating information about third-party explosions (for example, the joint crisis center) may be useful in managing a crisis that has already begun, but may not be very significant in preventing crises from arising in the first place. Moreover, they must be carefully designed to minimize their use for deception.

Because they often deal with less probable paths to nuclear war, or only with precipitating rather than deeper causes, CBMs are often treated as marginal in value and priority. It would be a mistake to ignore even such modest improvements in lowering nuclear risks. But it would be equally mistaken to constrain a strategy for nuclear risk reduction to measures that deal with the least likely paths (in Table 2-1), or only the precipitating rather than deeper causes (in the terms of Table 2-2). A serious strategy for nuclear risk reduction should work across the whole range of paths and proximity of causes. Those measures that deal with dangers of miscalculation between a closed and an open society should not be neglected simply because they are more political and less technical. On the other hand, particularly if there is a climate of deteriorating relations, it may be easier to start with more limited and technical measures. But such measures (e.g., the joint crisis control center) should be designed with an eye to their potential (perhaps subsequent) effect on broader and longer-term confidence-building measures. Similarly, arms control and other negotiations should be designed to give long-term transparency and communication considerations as prominent a priority as the signing of formal arms reduction treaties. In this broad sense of the term, CBMS and stabilization measures can play a significant role in a strategy of nuclear risk reduction.

NOTES

1. Stanley Hoffmann, *Primacy or World Order* (New York: McGraw Hill, 1978), p. 11; see also Michael Mandelbaum, *The Nuclear Revolution* (New York: Cambridge University Press, 1981), ch. 3.

2. See Robert Jervis, "Security Regimes," *International Organization* (Cambridge, Mass.: MIT Press, 1982).

3. Edwin S. Corwin, *The President: Office and Powers* (New York: N.Y.U. Press, 1940), 200.

4. This table was developed jointly with Albert Carnesale. For elaboration of scenarios, see A. Carnesale, P. Doty, S. Hoffmann, S. Huntington, J. Nye, S. Sagan, *Living With Nuclear Weapons* (New York: Bantam, 1983), ch. 3.

5. See J. J. Holst, "Confidence Building Measures: A Conceptual Framework," *Survival* (January/February 1983), p. 2. Holst defines CBMS as "arrangements designed to enhance . . . assurance of mind and belief in the trustworthiness of states and the facts they create." He argues that they "affect the margins of international conflict, they do not address the core."

6. Alexander George, "Third Areas Competition: Problems of Crisis Management and Crisis Prevention." in J. S. Nye (ed.), *American Democracy and Russian Reality,* Yale University Press (forthcoming).

7. This idea was suggested by Robert MacNamara.

8. *Report to the Congress by Secretary of Defense Caspar Weinberger on Direct Communication Links and Other Measures to Enhance Stability* (Washington: Department of Defense, April 11, 1983); reproduced in Appendix B.

9. Sam Nunn, "Arms Control: What Should We Do?" *Washington Post,* November 12, 1981.

10. I. William Zartman, "The Strategy of Preventive Diplomacy in Third World Conflicts," in Alexander George (ed.), *Managing U.S.-Soviet Rivalry* (Boulder: Westview Press, 1983), p. 362.

11. Richard Betts, *Surprise Attack* (Washington: Brookings, 1982), p. 306.

12. See Paul Gordon Lauren, "Crisis Prevention in Nineteenth-Century Diplomacy," in A. George (ed.) cited.

13. See Barry Blechman, Janne Nolan, and Alan Platt, "Negotiated Limits on Arms Transfers: First Steps Towards Crisis Prevention?" in A. George, cited.

14. See J. Nye, "The Future of Arms Control," Barry Blechman (ed.), *Rethinking the U.S. Strategic Posture* (Cambridge: Ballinger Publishing Company, 1982).

3 | Existing U.S.-Soviet Confidence-Building Measures

William J. Lynn

SINCE WORLD WAR II, the United States and the Soviet Union have participated in more than twenty international agreements, conventions, and treaties that have included measures to help manage crises or to build each state's confidence that the other does not intend to initiate conflict. Appendix 3-1 lists those agreements in chronological order, summarizing their relevant provisions and providing a brief explanation of how each has operated. The vast majority of the agreements were negotiated in the period between the Cuban Missile Crisis in 1963 and the Soviet invasion of Afghanistan in 1979. As the matrix in Table 3-1 illustrates, the agreements contain two broad classes of confidence-building measures: (1) restrictions on military activities and (2) instruments to facilitate the exchange of information regarding potentially threatening activities.

RESTRICTIONS ON MILITARY ACTIVITIES

Confidence-building measures have included five broad types of restrictions on military activities. The two most prominent are measures to restrict the capabilities of the two nations to wage nuclear war, through either bans on whole classes of weapons or limits on the size of nuclear arsenals. Toxin and bacteriological weapons have been outlawed in the 1972 Biological Weapons Convention. Similarly, the 1972 ABM Treaty restricts antiballistic missile systems so severely that in

Table 3-1
Existing U.S.-Soviet Confidence-Building Measures

	Restrictions on Military Activities						Informational Confidence-Building Measures			
	Ban on Class of Weapon	Numerical Limits	Regional Demilitarization	Non-Proliferation	Limits on Testing	General Conduct Limits	Special Comm. Links	Mutual Inspections	Notification Rqmts	Implementing Body
UN Military Staff										X
Berlin Agreement										X
Antarctica Treaty			X	X	X			X		
Hot Line Agreement							X			
Limited Test Ban					X					
Outer Space Treaty			X	X	X			X		X
Treaty of Tlatelolco			X	X	X			X		X
Non-Proliferation Treaty				X	X			X		X
Seabed Arms Control			X	X	X			X		X
Nuclear Accident Agmt.							X		X	X
Biological Weapons Conv.	X				X					X
Space Cooperation Agmt.										
Incidents at Sea Agmt.						X			X	
U.S.-Soviet Basic Principles Agmt.						X				
ABM Treaty	X									X
SALT I		X								X
Prevention of Nuclear War						X				
Threshold Test Ban					X					
CSCE									X	X
PNE Treaty					X			X	X	X
Envrnmtl Modification					X			X		X
SALT II		X							X	X

essence it too bans an entire class of weapons. The size of U.S. and Soviet strategic nuclear arsenals were limited by the two strategic arms limitation treaties: the SALT I Interim Agreement (1972) and the un-ratified SALT II Treaty (1979).

Four other types of restrictions on military activities have received less public attention. First, there have been agreements to demilitarize certain regions. The most comprehensive agreement in this category is the Antarctic Treaty (1959) banning all measures of a military nature on that continent. Several other treaties seek primarily to limit the spread of nuclear weapons into areas as yet free of them. The Outer Space Treaty (1967) bars the stationing of weapons of mass destruction in space or on celestial bodies. This treaty also prohibits the establish-ment of military installations, the conduct of military maneuvers, and the testing of any weapon on celestial bodies. The Seabed Arms Control Treaty (1971) bars the emplacement of nuclear weapons on the seabed or ocean floor outside the twelve-mile coastal zone. Finally, the most ambitious agreement in this regard is the Treaty of Tlatelolco (1967), which establishes a nuclear-weapon-free zone in Latin America.

Second, closely related to efforts to demilitarize regions, there are efforts to control the spread of nuclear weapons. In addition to the four agreements just cited, nonproliferation agreements include the Non-Proliferation Treaty (1968) forbidding its nonnuclear signatories from developing or acquiring nuclear weapons.

Third, there have been numerous efforts to limit the testing of nuclear weapons. The four agreements that seek to demilitarize certain areas, as well as the Non-Proliferation Treaty, all contain provisions prohibiting nuclear testing. There have also been three treaties that limit nuclear testing directly. The Limited Nuclear Test Ban (1963) bans all nuclear explosions in the atmosphere, outer space, and under-water. The Threshold Test Ban Treaty (1974) restricts all U.S. and Soviet nuclear testing below a 150-kiloton threshold, and the Peaceful Nuclear Explosion Treaty (1976) establishes yield limits and geo-graphic restrictions on peaceful nuclear explosions. The United States has not ratified either of the latter two treaties, although both the United States and the Soviet Union claim to be abiding by them.

Finally, the United States and the Soviet Union have negotiated several agreements that seek in effect to establish a code of conduct for their bilateral relations. These agreements fall into two categories.

First, there are general agreements such as the Agreement on Basic Principles of Relations (1972), which sought to establish a basis for peaceful bilateral relations, and the U.S.-Soviet Agreement on the Prevention of Nuclear War (1973), which called for both parties to act in such a manner as to exclude the outbreak of nuclear war. These two agreements are products of the most optimistic period of détente. In fact, they have proved to have little meaning or existence independent of the state of U.S.-Soviet relations. The second category of agreements restricts more specific types of activities and is generally thought to be more successful. The most notable example is the Incidents at Sea Agreement (1972), which specified rules of conduct for U.S. and Soviet naval ships. Both parties have stated their satisfaction with this agreement.

INFORMATIONAL CONFIDENCE-BUILDING MEASURES

This second class of confidence-building measures seeks to manage crises and build confidence by exchanging information about military activities. A few agreements, such as the Hot Line Agreement (1963) and the Nuclear Accidents Agreement (1971), have been free-standing attempts to facilitate the exchange of information. In most cases, however, the information exchanges have been intended to support broader agreements restricting military activities, such as the SALT agreements and the various nonproliferation treaties. These agreements have included three specific measures: mutual rights of inspection, requirements for notification of certain actions, and establishment of joint implementing bodies.

Mutual rights of inspection have been most prominent in the treaties restricting the proliferation of nuclear weapons. The Antarctic Treaty grants parties the right to inspect all areas of Antarctica, including stations, equipment, ships, and aircraft. Several parties, including the United States, have exercised this right of inspection. The Outer Space Treaty allows inspection of all facilities on celestial bodies on the basis of reciprocity. The Seabed Arms Control Treaty calls for verification to be accomplished by unilateral observation. Inspections are permitted only if all parties involved consent. Under the Non-Proliferation Treaty, the International Atomic Energy Agency (IAEA) inspects the nuclear facilities of consenting parties to ensure compliance with safeguard provisions.

Inspections are also used as a confidence-building measure in two agreements not related directly to nonproliferation efforts. To supplement national technical means of verification, the Peaceful Nuclear Explosions Treaty allows for exchanges of observers at the tests of nuclear devices intended for peaceful purposes. Since the United States has not ratified the treaty, these provisions never have been called into play. The confidence-building measures contained in the Final Act of the 1975 Conference on Security and Cooperation in Europe (CSCE) include voluntary measures for attendance of observers at military maneuvers. Western, as well as neutral and nonaligned, states have invited a cross section of observers to attend the majority of their maneuvers. Warsaw Pact states invited Western observers to maneuvers in the late 1970s but discontinued the practice after 1979.

A second category of measures used to build confidence in the context of treaties limiting military activities are requirements to notify the other parties of certain militarily significant actions, such as military maneuvers or weapons tests. The major confidence-building measure contained in the CSCE was the requirement to give twenty-one days notice of all military maneuvers involving more than 25,000 ground troops. Similarly, mutual notification provisions are at the core of the Nuclear Accidents Agreement between the United States and the Soviet Union. Under the agreement, each side pledged to notify the other in three specific cases: any accidental, unauthorized, or unexplained nuclear explosion; detection by missile warning systems of unidentified objects or interference with the warning systems; and planned missile launches beyond national territory in the direction of the other party. Similarly, the SALT II Treaty requires advance notification of certain missile launches. SALT II also calls for the United States and the USSR to maintain an agreed data base for systems limited by the treaty. Since the United States has not ratified the treaty, the provisions regarding the data base and the missile test notifications have not come into force. The Incidents at Sea Agreement requires the United States and the Soviet Union to give notification of actions on the high seas that represent a danger to navigation or to aircraft in flight. Finally, both the Threshold Test Ban Treaty and the Peaceful Nuclear Explosion Treaty call for each side to notify the other prior to testing nuclear devices, as well as to provide certain data regarding the test. Again, since these treaties have not been ratified, the notifications and data exchanges have never taken place.

The third category of procedural confidence-building measures, establishment of joint implementing bodies, is by far the most prevalent. The most prominent joint implementing body is the Standing Consultative Commission (SCC). The SCC was established to promote the objectives of the ABM Treaty, the SALT I Interim Agreement, and the Nuclear Accidents Agreement. The SALT II Treaty also incorporates the SCC by reference. The SCC meets twice each year to consider questions concerning treaty compliance and verification, as well as any desired modifications. In this context, the SCC has completed protocols on the dismantling of nuclear weapons and ABMs, conducted two reviews of the ABM Treaty, and established preagreed messages to be sent on the hot line in case of a nuclear accident.

Both the United States and the Soviet Union also have raised a number of issues within the SCC regarding compliance with the ABM, SALT I, and SALT II agreements. In 1979, the United States Arms Control and Disarmament Agency (ACDA) reported that all United States questions had been resolved satisfactorily—the Soviets either ceased the activity or additional information allayed United States concerns. In 1984, however, ACDA cataloged seven possible Soviet violations of SALT I, the ABM Treaty, and SALT II. These United States concerns have not yet been resolved. Moreover, there apparently has been an internal debate within the Reagan Administration as to whether the United States should raise these, and possibly others, alleged violations in the SCC.

There are several other examples of agreements establishing joint implementing bodies as confidence-building measures. On the model of the SCC, the unratified Peaceful Nuclear Explosion Treaty calls for establishment of a Joint Consultative Commission to consider questions of compliance and verification. The Non-Proliferation Treaty employs the IAEA as a permanent implementing body. The Berlin Air Corridor Agreement (1946) created the Berlin Air Space Center, which serves as clearing center for Western aircraft entering the Berlin air corridors.

Three multilateral agreements—the Seabed Arms Control Treaty, the Biological Weapons Convention, and the Environmental Modification Convention—employ the United Nations Security Council as an implementing body. Parties refer complaints to the Security Council, which may then authorize a Commission of Experts to investigate. A UN Commission of Experts investigated U.S. charges that the Soviet Union or its allies had violated the Biological Weapons Convention by using toxin weapons in Afghanistan and Southeast Asia. The Commission, however, was unable either to substantiate or to disprove the accusations.

Finally, undoubtedly the least successful implementing body has been the UN Military Staff Committee. Article 47 of the United Nations Charter established the Military Staff Committee to advise and assist the Security Council on questions regarding the use of UN military forces, as well as disarmament issues. Although it meets twice a month, the Military Staff Committee has not deliberated on any substantive matter in over 37 years.

CONCLUSION

There are substantial precedents for employing confidence-building measures to reduce the risk of nuclear confrontations between the United States and the Soviet Union, on both a bilateral and a multi-lateral basis. Most of the existing bilateral agreements that include confidence-building measures have dealt with limits on the testing of nuclear devices and, more generally, on restricting the size and the capabilities of the two sides' nuclear arsenals. At the beginning of the 1970s, during the height of détente, there were also some largely unsuccessful efforts to set forth basic principles to govern relations between the United States and the Soviet Union. The dominant objective of multilateral agreements that contain confidence-building measures has been to restrict the further proliferation of nuclear weapons. Both bilateral and multilateral agreements have focused on three types of informational confidence-building measures: mutual inspection provisions, notification requirements, and establishment of joint implementing bodies.

APPENDIX 3-1—CATALOG OF EXISTING U.S.-SOVIET CRISIS MANAGEMENT AND CONFIDENCE-BUILDING MEASURES

UN Military Staff Committee

Charter of the United Nations, Article 47

Signed: June 26, 1945
Entered into Force: October 24, 1945
Members: U.S., USSR, U.K., France, and China

Duration: Not specified
Relevant Provisions

Article 47 of the UN Charter calls for the establishment of a Military Staff Committee to advise and assist the Security Council on all questions relating to military requirements for the maintenance of international peace and security, the employment and command of forces placed at Security Council disposal, the regulation of armaments, and possible disarmament. The membership of the Military Staff Committee consists of a representative from each of the five permanent members of the Security Council.

History of Compliance

The Staff Committee's first assignment from the Security Council was its last. For nearly fifteen months in 1946–47, it debated without reaching agreement the force structure and composition of UN military forces for collective security. Since that time the Staff Committee has remained in existence, meeting briefly twice monthly to take attendance and adjourn. It has not deliberated on any substantive matter in over thirty-seven years.

Berlin Air Corridor Agreement

Flight Rules by Allied Control Authority Air Directorate for Aircraft Flying in Air Corridors in Germany and Berlin Control Zone

Signed: October 22, 1946
Entered into Force: October 22, 1946
Parties: U.S., USSR, U.K., and France
Duration: Not specified
Relevant Provisions

This agreement sets forth flight rules and safety measures for the three air corridors to Berlin and for the airspace around Berlin itself. To regulate flight in these corridors, the agreement establishes the Berlin Air Space Center (BASC), consisting of air controllers from each of the four Occupying Powers.

History of Compliance

BASC functions as a clearing center for Western aircraft entering the Berlin air corridors. In practice, Western air controllers inform the Soviet air controller when Western aircraft enter the air corridors and the Soviet controller then informs the Soviet military command. Similarly, Western complaints about Soviet actions in the air corridors are transmitted through the BASC.

On September 3, 1971, the four Occupying Powers signed the Quadripartite Agreement on Berlin which resolved questions concerning the flow of civilian ground traffic to West Berlin and the relationship of West Berlin to the Federal Republic of Germany. Although this agreement did not address air traffic to Berlin (which the 1946 Air Corridor Agreement has continued to govern), it confirmed the removal of Berlin as a major flash point in East-West relations. Accordingly, since 1971, incidents in the air corridors have been few and the operations of BASC have gone smoothly. Currently, BASC is one of the two remaining quadripartite bodies in Berlin—the other is Spandau Prison where Rudolf Hess is incarcerated.

Antarctica Treaty
Signed: December 1, 1959
Entered into Force: June 23, 1961
Parties: Twelve signatories including U.S. and USSR
Duration: Unlimited (with provision for review after thirty years)
Relevant Provisions

The treaty provides that Antarctica shall be used for peaceful purposes only. It specifically prohibits any measures of a military nature such as the establishment of military bases, the testing of weapons, or the conduct of military maneuvers. Parties have the right to inspect all areas of Antarctica including all stations, equipment, ships, and aircraft. The treaty also provides for regular consultative meetings of the contracting parties to discuss measures to further the objectives of the treaty.

History of Compliance

Argentina, Australia, New Zealand, the United Kingdom, and the United States have all exercised the right of inspection. American inspections have taken place on a biannual basis; and all inspections have included Soviet facilities. None of the inspections have discovered any prohibited activities. The observed activities at each station were in compliance with the provisions and the spirit of the treaty.

Eleven consultative meetings have been held, the most recent in 1981.

Hot Line Agreement
Memorandum of Understanding Between the United States of America and the Union of Soviet Socialist Republics Regarding the Establishment of a Direct Communications Link

Signed: June 20, 1963
Entered into Force: June 20, 1963
Parties: U.S. and USSR
Duration: Not specified

Relevant Provisions

The Hot Line Agreement established a direct communications link between the governments of the United States and the Soviet Union for use in time of emergency. An annex to the agreement provided for two full-time circuits—a wire telegraph circuit and a radio telegraph circuit as a backup—as well as two terminal points with telegraph-teleprinter equipment.

In 1971, the United States and the USSR agreed to modernize the communication link with satellite circuits and a system of multiple terminals. When the satellite circuits became operational in 1978, the radio telegraph circuit was terminated. The wire telegraph circuit has been retained as a backup, however.

In July 1984, the United States and the Soviet Union initialed a diplomatic note, agreeing to further upgrade the "hot line." The agreement called for a facsimile transmission capability to be added to the existing system, permitting faster transmissions and the inclusion of graphic material such as maps and charts.

History of Compliance

The communications link has proved its value several times since its installation. For example, during the 1967 Arab-Israeli War, the United States employed the "hot line" to avoid possible Soviet mis-understandings of American fleet movements in the Mediterranean. The United States also used the "hot line" during the 1971 Indo-Pakistani War. Moscow used the link during the 1973 Arab-Israeli War to convey its displeasure with the United States' inability to induce Israel to accept a ceasefire.

Limited Test Ban Treaty
Treaty Banning Nuclear Weapon Tests in the Atmosphere, in Outer Space, and Under Water

Signed: August 5, 1963
Entered into Force: October 10, 1963
Parties: 106 signatories including the U.S. and USSR
Duration: Unlimited

Relevant Provisions

The Limited Test Ban Treaty prohibits all nuclear explosions in the atmosphere, outer space, under water, or in any environment that would cause radioactive debris to escape the territorial limits of the nation conducting the test. The preamble to the treaty stated that a discontinuance of all nuclear tests for all time was the goal of the parties. Since the parties assumed that national technical means of verification would be sufficient, the treaty includes no provisions for verification.

History of Compliance

All signatories have apparently complied with the treaty, but two nuclear powers—China and France—have not signed it and each has conducted atmospheric tests since 1963. In September 1979, a U.S. satellite detected a flash of light over the South Atlantic with the characteristics of flashes that accompany nuclear explosions. No corroborating evidence was found. Whether it was a nuclear explosion and, if so, which nation was responsible remains uncertain.

Treaty of Tlatelolco

Treaty for the Prohibition of Nuclear Weapons in Latin America

Signed: February 14, 1967
Entered into Force: April 22, 1968
Parties: Twenty-five Latin American states (U.S. and USSR have
    signed relevant Protocol)
Duration: Indefinite

Relevant Provisions

The Treaty of Tlatelolco establishes a nuclear-weapon-free zone in Latin America. Under the treaty, all parties agree not to test, use, acquire, or manufacture nuclear weapons. In return for this voluntary abstention from the nuclear club, the treaty has two additional protocols that provide Latin American states with certain pledges and assurances from outside powers. Under Protocol I, outside states with territories in Latin America agree to apply the treaty provisions to those territories. Of the four outside powers with territory in the region, the Netherlands, the United Kingdom and the United States have signed and ratified the Protocol, while France has signed but not ratified it. Protocol II calls for all nuclear-weapon states to respect the nuclear-free status of the zone and to refrain from making nuclear threats against Latin American treaty members. All five nuclear-weapon states, including the United States and the Soviet Union, have signed and ratified this Protocol.

History of Compliance

This is the first and, thus far, the only treaty creating a nuclear-free zone in a major populated area. The treaty, however, does not come into force until two conditions are met: all Latin American states have signed and ratified it, and all relevant outside powers have signed and ratified the two protocols. Signatories, however, can waive these conditions, in which case the treaty enters into force for their territory immediately on deposit of their instrument of ratification. At present, the treaty is in force for twenty-two Latin American nations. But the remaining states include the most crucial. Brazil and Chile have signed and ratified the treaty, but have not waived the conditions to bring it into force. Argentina has signed but not ratified the treaty, despite repeated promises to do so. Finally, Cuba refuses to sign the treaty until a series of conditions have been met, including removal of all foreign military bases from Latin America (particularly the U.S. naval base at Guantánamo), termination of the U.S. economic embargo against Cuba, and assurances from all nuclear-weapon states that they will not subject Latin American states to any kind of coercion—political, economic, or military.

Although the treaty has arguably made a contribution to regional nonproliferation, it has had a minimal impact on superpower activities in Latin America. The fact that there have been no repetitions of the Cuban Missile Crisis is attributable not to the treaty, but to the mutual desire of the superpowers to avoid such dangerous situations. Since the crisis, the United States and the Soviet Union have combined on a series of arms control and confidence-building measures to regulate their nuclear competition more effectively. With regard to the specific issue of superpower deployment of nuclear weapons in Latin America, the treaty at best ratifies a decision that the United States and the Soviet Union already had taken bilaterally. The United States never has had any incentive to station nuclear weapons in Latin America. All potential U.S. targets and opponents lie elsewhere; and in any event the United States maintains a dominant conventional arms presence. Although the Soviet Union could conceivably gain some leverage in its strategic competition with the United States by deploying nuclear weapons in Latin America, Moscow tacitly agreed to forgo such deployments as part of the resolution of the missile crisis. The Treaty of Tlatelolco contributes only marginally, if at all, to this tacit superpower denuclearization of Latin America. This is especially true in light of the fact that Cuba, still the most likely base for any Soviet nuclear weapons, refuses to sign the treaty.

Outer Space Treaty

Treaty on Principles Governing the Activities of States in the Exploration and Use of Outer Space, Including the Moon and Other Celestial Bodies

Ratified by U.S.: May 24, 1967
Entered into Force: October 10, 1967
Parties: Eighty-nine signatories including the U.S. and USSR
Duration: Not specified

Relevant Provisions

The treaty lays down principles governing peaceful activities of states in outer space, restricting military activities in space in two ways. First, the parties undertake not to place in orbit around the Earth, install on the moon or any other celestial body, or otherwise station in outer space nuclear or any other weapons of mass destruction. Second, the treaty prohibits the establishment of military installations, the conduct of military maneuvers, and the testing of any type of weapon on celestial bodies. Under the treaty, all stations, installations, equipment, and space vehicles on the moon or other celestial bodies are open to inspection by other parties on the basis of reciprocity.

History of Compliance

Subsequent to this treaty, several follow-up agreements on technical and legal aspects of space exploration and use were signed: The Agreement on the Rescue of Astronauts, the Return of Astronauts, and the Return of Objects Launched into Outer Space (1968); the Convention for International Liability for Damage Caused by Space Objects (1973); and the Convention on Registration of Objects Launched into Outer Space (1976). This last Convention calls for the Secretary General of the UN to maintain a registry of space objects which lists the launching state, the date and location of the launch, the basic orbital parameters of the space object, and its general function. Under the Convention, this information is to be provided by the launching state.

The Outer Space Treaty has not reduced either nation's efforts to develop space weaponry. Since most space weapons under consideration—particle beams, laser weapons, and antisatellite weapons—do not cause mass destruction and would be placed in orbit rather than on some celestial body, they are not prohibited under the Outer Space Treaty.

Non-Proliferation Treaty
Treaty on the Non-Proliferation of Nuclear Weapons

Signed: July 1, 1968
Entered into Force: March 5, 1970
Parties: Ninety-seven signatories including the U.S. and USSR
Duration: Twenty-five years, at which time a conference will be held to determine if it should continue indefinitely or be extended for an additional term

Relevant Provisions

The Non-Proliferation Treaty (NPT) forbids nuclear powers from transferring nuclear weapons to non-nuclear states. Non-nuclear parties to the NPT also foreswear development or acquisition of nuclear weapons. All parties to the treaty, however, are to have full access to materials and information for peaceful uses of nuclear energy. The safeguard provisions of the treaty, which are implemented by the International Atomic Energy Agency (IAEA), apply only to the non-nuclear parties. However, in 1977, the United States voluntarily concluded an agreement with the IAEA that submitted U.S. nonweapons nuclear facilities to IAEA inspection. In 1982, Moscow announced its readiness to put some of its nuclear powerplants under IAEA safeguards and is actively negotiating the detailed arrangements with the IAEA.

History of Compliance

Although the effectiveness of the NPT in halting proliferation has been questioned, the U.S. and the USSR have not had any major disputes over nonproliferation issues. Indeed, Moscow and Washington have cooperated on proliferation issues at NPT Review Conferences, IAEA meetings, and UN General Assembly sessions on proliferation issues, as well as in the London Suppliers Group. This cooperation was further demonstrated in 1977 when Moscow observed what were thought to be preparations for a nuclear explosion in South Africa and relayed the information to Washington.

Seabed Arms Control Treaty
Treaty on the Prohibition of Nuclear Weapons and Other Weapons of Mass Destruction on the Seabed and the Ocean Floor and in the Subsoil Thereof

Signed: February 11, 1971
Entered into Force: May 18, 1972
Parties: Eighty-seven signatories including U.S. and USSR
Duration: Not specified (provision for periodic review conferences)
Relevant Provisions
The treaty prohibits the emplacement of nuclear weapons or other weapons of mass destruction in the seabed or on the ocean floor beyond the twelve-mile coastal zone. Verification is accomplished by unilateral observation. More intrusive measures, such as inspection of facilities, are subject to the agreement of all parties involved. Parties may refer complaints to the UN Security Council.
History of Compliance
The initial treaty review conference in 1977 concluded that the first five years of the treaty had demonstrated its effectiveness. There have been no allegations of violations during the treaty's ten years of existence.

Nuclear Accidents Agreement
Agreement on Measures to Reduce the Risk of Outbreak of Nuclear War Between the United States of America and the Union of Soviet Socialist Republics

Signed: September 30, 1971
Entered into Force: September 30, 1971
Parties: U.S. and USSR
Duration: Unlimited
Relevant Provisions
The agreement consists of a series of measures designed to reduce the risk of nuclear war as the result of unintended, unauthorized, or misinterpreted actions. The measures include:

1. A mutual pledge to undertake measures to maintain and improve organizational and technical safeguards against accidental or unauthorized use of nuclear weapons
2. Immediate notification in the case of an accidental, unauthorized,

or other unexplained incident involving the possible detonation of a nuclear weapon; (the Party whose weapon is involved would also attempt to render harmless or destroy the errant weapon)

3. Immediate notification of detection by missile warning systems of unidentified objects or interference with the warning systems themselves, if either occurrence could create the risk of nuclear war

4. Advance notification of planned missile launches that extend beyond national territory and in the direction of the other party

5. Agreement to use the "hot line" for transmission of urgent information, notifications, and requests for information in situations requiring prompt clarification

History of Compliance

Except for the provisions regarding notification of certain missile launches (to which both sides have adhered), the procedures set forth in this agreement have never been called into play. The two sides, however, have worked out certain preagreed messages to be relayed over the "hot line" in case of a nuclear accident. These arrangements were negotiated in the Standing Consultative Commission. (The 1977 Protocol on the Use of Immediate Notifications in Implementation of the Agreement on Measures.)

Biological Weapons Convention

Convention on the Prohibition of the Development, Production, and Stockpiling of Bacteriological (Biological) and Toxin Weapons and on Their Destruction

Signed: April 10, 1972
Entered into Force: March 26, 1975
Parties: 111 signatories including U.S. and USSR
Duration: Unlimited (with provisions for a review conference after five years)

Relevant Provisions

Each party to the Convention agreed not to develop, produce, or stockpile biological or toxin weapons and to destroy any existing stockpile of such weapons within nine months of the Convention entering into force. The treaty does not establish a specific monitoring mechanism or procedure, but provides that any party believing another to be in violation may lodge a complaint with the UN Security Council. The Security Council may then initiate an investigation and mandate assistance to parties exposed to danger as a result of a violation.

History of Compliance

After the Convention entered into force, the United States announced that it had destroyed its entire stockpile of biological and toxin weapons and converted its former biological warfare facilities to peaceful purposes. Similarly, the Soviet Union declared that it did not possess any bacteriological agents or toxins, weapons, equipment, or means of delivery as prohibited in the Convention.

A 1979 anthrax epidemic in the Soviet city of Sverdlovsk has raised questions about whether the Soviet Union continues to produce and stockpile biological weapons in violation of the Convention. Moreover, the United States, Canada, and other nations have charged that the USSR or its allies have used toxin weapons (as well as chemical weapons) in Southeast Asia and Afghanistan. Moscow has denied these charges. A UN Commission of Experts has been unable either to substantiate or to disprove the accusations.

Space Cooperation Agreement

Agreement Between the United States of America and the Union of Soviet Socialist Republics Concerning Cooperation in the Exploration and Use of Outer Space for Peaceful Purposes

Signed: May 24, 1972
Entered into Force: May 24, 1972
Parties: U.S. and USSR
Duration: Five years, renewed in 1977
Expired: May 24, 1982

Relevant Provisions

This agreement calls for Soviet-American cooperation in the fields of space meteorology, natural environment studies, space exploration, and space biology and medicine. This cooperation included establishment of joint working groups, participation in mutual exchanges of scientific information and delegations, and pursuit of a Soviet-American linkup in space. Many of the specifics of these cooperative arrangements had been established in an earlier agreement between the U.S. National Aeronautics and Space Administration and the Soviet Academy of Sciences (Summary of Results of Discussions on Space Cooperation Between the Academy of Sciences of the USSR and the U.S. National Aeronautics and Space Administration—1971).

History of Compliance

The Space Cooperation Agreement led to the 1975 Apollo-Soyuz linkup in space. The working groups of Soviet and American scientists that were established under the agreement fostered mutual assistance and information exchanges on a range of space issues. These working groups were disbanded when the Reagan Administration decided to allow the Space Cooperation Agreement to expire in 1982. Nevertheless, some low-level exchanges of data, work on joint publications, and work on joint projects still continue.

Incidents at Sea Agreement

American-Soviet Agreement on the Prevention of Incidents On and Over the High Seas

Signed: May 25, 1972
Entered into Force: May 25, 1972
Parties: U.S. and USSR
Duration: Three years with provision for self-renewal

Relevant Provisions

The agreement provides for measures to ensure the safety of navigation of American and Soviet warships on the high seas. It specifies rules of conduct for ships engaged in surveillance of other ships, as well as ships engaged in launching or landing aircraft. The parties also undertake to give notification of actions on the high seas that represent a danger to navigation or to aircraft in flight. Finally, the agreement bans ships and aircraft from harassing or simulating attacks on ships of the other Party. To review compliance with these provisions, the agreement calls for annual meetings between American and Soviet naval officers.

History of Compliance

In practice, each side has relayed complaints of violations of the agreement directly to the other party through its naval attaché. These complaints have then been reviewed and discussed at the annual meetings. In general, both Moscow and Washington have been satisfied with the operation of the agreement. Since 1972, the number of incidents at sea and their seriousness have lessened significantly, thus reducing a serious source of tension between the two powers.

ABM Treaty

Treaty Between the United States of America and the Union of Soviet
Socialist Republics on the Limitation of Anti-ballistic Missile Systems

Signed: May 26, 1972
Entered into Force: October 3, 1972
Parties: U.S. and USSR
Duration: Unlimited with five-year reviews

Relevant Provisions

Under the ABM Treaty, the United States and the Soviet Union
undertake not to deploy ABM systems intended for regional or national
defense. The treaty defines ABM as "a system to counter strategic
ballistic missiles or their elements in flight trajectory." Each side is
limited to two (later reduced to one) ABM deployment areas with 100
interceptor missiles each, located at least 1,300 kilometers apart to
prevent creation of a regional defense. The treaty sets out the number
and characteristics of the radars permitted at the designated ABM sites,
as well as the radius of the deployment area. It also limits qualitative
improvements in ABM technology, barring development, testing, or
deployment of multiple-launch and rapid-reload ABM systems and of
systems that are sea-based, air-based, space-based, or mobile land-
based.

To promote the objectives and implementation of the treaty, the
parties established the Standing Consultative Commission. (See the
SCC Memorandum following.) Compliance with the treaty is to be
assured by "national technical means of verification." Both parties
agree not to interfere with those means and not to use deliberate
measures of concealment to impede verification.

History of Compliance

For a decade after its signing, many observers considered the ABM
Treaty to be the most significant achievement of modern arms control.
More recently, two developments have raised questions about its
continued viability. First, the proliferation on both sides of phased-
array radars that might be used in an ABM mode and the development
on both sides of highly capable surface-to-air missiles that have potential capabilities against ballistic missiles appear to be undermining the
treaty's strict limits on ABM technology. Second, the Strategic Defense
Initiative of the Reagan Administration would, if pursued to the development and deployment of missile defenses, require the modification or abrogation of the ABM Treaty.

SALT I Interim Agreement
Interim Agreement Between the United States of America and the Union of Soviet Socialist Republics on Certain Measures with Respect to the Limitation of Strategic Offensive Arms

Signed: May 26, 1972
Entered into Force: October 3, 1972
Parties: U.S. and USSR
Duration: Five years

Relevant Provisions

The interim agreement provided essentially for a freeze of existing American and Soviet strategic nuclear arsenals, pending further negotiations. Both sides agreed not to construct additional intercontinental ballistic missile (ICBM) launchers. When the agreement took force, the United States had 1,054 ICBM launchers and the Soviet Union had 1,618. The agreement also limited modern ballistic missile submarines and launchers for submarine-launched ballistic missiles (SLBMS). Under the agreement, the United States was permitted to build up to a maximum of 710 SLBM launchers on 44 submarines from its existing force of 656 launchers on 41 submarines. Similarly, the Soviet Union could build its force from 710 launchers to a maximum of 950 launchers on 62 submarines. The additional SLBM launchers for both sides, however, were allowed only as replacements for older ballistic missile launchers.

The agreement stipulated that compliance was to be assured by "national technical means of verification." In this context, both sides agreed not to interfere with national technical means of verification and not to use deliberate concealment measures to impede verification. Finally, the SCC established under the ABM Treaty was to be used to promote the objectives and implementation of the agreement.

History of Compliance

The agreement expired in 1977 without the United States and the Soviet Union having agreed on further limitations. Both sides, however, announced that they intended to refrain from actions incompatible with the provisions and the objectives of the talks on a new strategic arms limitation agreement (SALT II). SALT II was signed but not ratified in 1979. (See section on SALT II below.)

U.S.-Soviet Agreement on Basic Principles of Relations

Agreement on Basic Principles of Relations Between the United States of America and the Union of Soviet Socialist Republics

Signed: May 29, 1972
Entered into Force: May 29, 1972
Parties: U.S. and USSR
Duration: Not specified

Relevant Provisions

The agreement declares that relations between the United States and the Soviet Union will be conducted on the basis of peaceful coexistence and mutual equality; that the two nations will continue to seek to limit armaments on a bilateral as well as a multilateral basis; that they will seek to avoid military confrontations and to prevent the outbreak of nuclear war; and that their ultimate objective is the achievement of general and complete disarmament and the establishment of an effective system of international security in accordance with the principles of the United Nations.

History of Compliance

This agreement has had no life independent of the general state of American-Soviet relations.

Standing Consultative Commission

American-Soviet Memorandum of Understanding Regarding the Establishment of a Standing Consultative Commission

Signed: December 21, 1972
Entered into Force: December 21, 1972
Parties: U.S. and USSR
Duration: Not specified

Relevant Provisions

The memorandum establishes a Standing Consultative Commission (SCC) to promote the objectives of the provisions of the ABM Treaty, the SALT I Interim Agreement, and the Nuclear Accidents Agreement. (The SALT II Treaty also incorporates the SCC by reference.) According to the SCC memorandum, each government is to be represented by a commissioner and a deputy commissioner, assisted by such staff as it deems necessary. The memorandum calls for a minimum of two SCC meetings per year, but the commissioners may communicate with each other between scheduled meetings. All proceedings of the meetings are to be private. The SCC mandate includes seven functions:

1. To consider questions concerning treaty compliance
2. To provide on a voluntary basis information necessary to ensure confidence in compliance
3. To consider questions involving unintended interference with national technical means of verification
4. To consider possible changes in the strategic situation that have a bearing on the provisions of the treaties
5. To agree upon procedures for replacement, conversion, dismantling, or destruction of strategic arms as called for in the treaties
6. To consider amendments and proposals for further increasing the viability of the treaties
7. To consider proposals for further limiting strategic arms

The SCC is also the forum for maintenance of the agreed data base on strategic offensive systems called for in SALT II.

History of Compliance

The SCC has met at least twice per year since its first meeting in 1973, dealing with a wide range of topics involving all relevant treaties. In 1974, the SCC completed two protocols on procedures governing the replacement, dismantling, or destruction of strategic offensive arms and of ABM systems. In 1976, the two SCC commissioners signed a supplementary protocol regulating the replacement of ABM systems and the exchange of ABM system deployment areas. The first ABM Treaty review was conducted by the SCC in 1977 and the second review was conducted by the SCC during the fall of 1982.

With regard to the Nuclear Accidents Agreement, the SCC agreed to the Protocol on the Use of Immediate Notifications in Implementation of the Agreement on Measures which established preagreed messages to be sent on the "hot line" in case of a nuclear accident.

Finally, the SCC has considered questions raised by both sides regarding compliance with the SALT I agreements. The Soviet side has raised questions about the following U.S. activities:

Shelters over Minuteman silos
Status of Atlas and Titan I launchers
Radar on Shemya Island
Privacy of SCC proceedings
Dismantling or destruction of ABM radar under construction at Malmstorm Air Force Base
Various radar deployments

The United States has raised questions about the following Soviet activities:

Identification of special-purpose silos of launch-control facilities
Concealment measures
Modern large ballistic missiles
Possible testing of an air defense system (SA-5) in an ABM mode
Reporting of dismantling of excess ABM test launchers
ABM radar on Kamchatka Peninsula
Dismantling or destruction of replaced ICBM launchers
Concealment at a test range

In each instance, according to a 1979 ACDA report, the Soviet activity in question had either ceased or additional information had allayed U.S. concerns.

In 1984, however, ACDA cataloged seven possible Soviet violations of SALT I, the ABM Treaty, and SALT II. These U.S. concerns have not yet been resolved. Moreover, there apparently has been some disagreement within the Reagan Administration itself as to whether the United States should raise these, and possibly other, alleged violations in the SCC.

Agreement on the Prevention of Nuclear War
Agreement Between the United States of America and the Union of Soviet Socialist Republics on the Prevention of Nuclear War

Signed: June 22, 1973
Entered into Force: June 22, 1973
Parties: U.S. and USSR
Duration: Unlimited
  Relevant Provisions
  The agreement provides that the parties will act in such a manner as to exclude the outbreak of nuclear war between them or between either of the parties and other countries. Each party will refrain from the threat or use of force against the other party, its allies, or other countries in circumstances that may endanger international peace and security. Finally, the parties agree that in a situation that involves the risk of nuclear confrontation—either between the United States and the USSR or between one of them and other countries—the parties will consult with each other to avoid this risk.

History of Compliance

No formal consultations have taken place under the provisions of this agreement, although Nixon did make reference to the agreement in a message to Brezhnev during the 1973 Middle East crisis.

Threshold Test Ban Treaty

Treaty Between the United States of America and the Union of Soviet Socialist Republics on the Limitation of Underground Nuclear Weapon Tests (and Protocol Thereto)

Signed: July 3, 1974
Not in force (Both sides, however, have stated that they are abiding by the treaty's terms)
Parties: U.S. and USSR
Duration: Five years with provisions for self-renewal

Relevant Provisions

The treaty establishes a nuclear threshold by prohibiting nuclear weapon tests having a yield greater than 150 kilotons. The nations are to verify compliance to the treaty using national technical means supplemented by data exchanges. The Protocol to the treaty details the data that will be exchanged, including information on the geography and geology of the test sites and the yield, depth, and coordinates of several tests for calibration purposes. After the treaty was signed, the two sides agreed to an addendum regarding how to treat slight, un-intended breaches of the 150-kiloton limit: one or two such breaches per year would not be considered a violation *per se*, but might be cause for consultation between the parties. The reason for this addendum to the treaty is that it is difficult to assess precisely the explosive force of underground blasts.

History of Compliance

The United States has not ratified the treaty. The Reagan Administration has requested the Senate to suspend consideration of it until the administration has devised measures to strengthen the verification provisions. Nevertheless, both the United States and the Soviet Union have claimed to adhere to the treaty since March 31, 1976—the date it was to take effect. Neither side has provided the other with the data on tests called for by the treaty. Despite Moscow's protestations to the contrary, some observers contend that several post–1976 Soviet tests have exceeded the 150-kiloton threshold.

Confidence-Building Measures in Europe
Document on Confidence-Building Measures and Certain Aspects of
Security and Disarmament, Included in the Final Act of the Conference
on Security and Cooperation in Europe

Signed: August 1, 1975
Entered into Force: August 1, 1975
Parties: Thirty-five signatories including U.S. and USSR
Duration: Not specified

Relevant Provisions

The signatories to the Helsinki Final Act committed themselves to
giving twenty-one days notice of all maneuvers involving more than
25,000 ground troops. The agreement also provides for notification on
a discretionary basis of maneuvers below the 25,000-troop threshold
and of major military movements. Finally, the signatories may on a
voluntary basis invite other participating states to send observers to
attend military maneuvers.

History of Compliance

All parties appear to have abided by the letter of the agreement on
confidence-building measures in Europe, although the spirit has been
lacking on the discretionary provisions—particularly among Warsaw
Pact nations. No state has failed to provide notification of maneuvers
involving more than 25,000 troops (although Moscow apparently
failed to supply the required information about the size of the maneuvers when notifying its "Zapad-81" exercise).

Western states and neutral and nonaligned states have announced
some maneuvers below the 25,000-troop threshold. In the Warsaw
Pact, only Hungary has notified any such maneuvers and then with
very short warning. No state has notified either major military movements or independent air force and navy exercises. With regard to
observers, Western states and neutral and nonaligned states have invited a cross section of states to send observers to the majority of their
maneuvers. Initially, Warsaw Pact states invited only observers from
neighboring states. In the late 1970s, they expanded their invitations to
include more Western observers. The Western observers complained,
however, that they had few opportunities to observe the actual maneuvers, rather than staged performances. The Warsaw Pact nations
have not invited any Western observers since 1979.

Peaceful Nuclear Explosion Treaty
Treaty Between the United States of America and the Union of Soviet Socialist Republics on Underground Nuclear Explosions for Peaceful Purposes (and Protocol Thereto)

Signed: May 28, 1976
Parties: U.S. and USSR
Not in force (same status as the Threshold Test Ban Treaty)
Duration: Five years with provisions for self-renewal

Relevant Provisions

The PNE Treaty governs all nuclear explosions carried out at locations other than the weapon test sites specified under the Threshold Test Ban Treaty. For such explosions, the PNE establishes a yield limit of 150 kilotons on individual tests, and 1,500 kilotons on group tests (provided each individual explosion in the group test can be identified and is itself less than 150 kilotons). The treaty calls for national technical means of verification to be supplemented by an exchange of information and observers. The Protocol to the treaty specifies the details of this supplementary verification. For group explosions with a total yield exceeding 150 kilotons, the Protocol requires the parties to invite observers. Observers are optional for group and individual explosions in the 100- to 150-kiloton range. Finally, the PNE Treaty calls for establishment of a Joint Consultative Commission to discuss the details of compliance, to consider questions of unintended interference with verification, and to develop further the details of the on-site inspection process.

History of Compliance

The status of the PNE Treaty is identical to that of the Threshold Test Ban Treaty. (see above).

Environmental Modification Convention
Convention on the Prohibition of Military or Any Other Hostile Use of Environmental Modification Techniques

Signed: May 18, 1977
Entered into Force: October 5, 1978
Parties: Forty-eight signatories including U.S. and USSR
Duration: Unlimited (with provisions for review conferences at five-year intervals)

Relevant Provisions

Each party to the convention undertakes not to engage in military or any other hostile use of environmental modification techniques having widespread, long-lasting, or severe effects as the means of destruction, damage, or injury to any other party. In addition to provisions for mutual consultation regarding complaints and for recourse to the UN Security Council, the Convention establishes a framework for convening a Consultative Committee of Experts. The Committee would meet on an *ad hoc* basis, when so requested by a party to investigate alleged violations of the convention.

History of Compliance

This convention has been uncontroversial since environmental modification techniques do not play a major role in military planning at the present time. No party has yet requested the convening of a Consultative Committee of Experts.

SALT II

Treaty Between the United States of America and the Union of Soviet Socialist Republics on the Limitation of Strategic Offensive Arms

Signed: June 18, 1979
Not in Force (Both sides, however, have stated that they are abiding by the treaty's terms)
Parties: U.S. and USSR
Duration: Expires December 31, 1985

Relevant Provisions

The SALT II accord includes a number of agreements: the treaty itself, a protocol on cruise missiles, a series of agreed statements and common understandings, an agreed data base, a Soviet statement on the Backfire bomber, and a joint statement of principles and guidelines for subsequent negotiations on strategic weapons. The main provisions of the treaty establish equal ceilings on the number of strategic delivery vehicles—ICBM launchers, SLBM launchers, and heavy bombers. Within an aggregate limit of 2,400 delivery vehicles, the treaty establishes a series of sublimits on launchers of multiple, independently targetable reentry vehicles (MIRVs): 1,320 launchers of MIRVed ballistic missiles and heavy bombers equipped with long-range cruise missiles, 1,200 launchers of MIRVed ballistic missiles, and 820 launchers of MIRVed ICBMS. SALT II also establishes limits on the development of new types of strategic nuclear weapons. Most importantly in this regard, it limits both parties to development of one new ICBM.

Both parties agreed not to circumvent the provisions of the agreement. Verification was to be accomplished by national technical means. The treaty prohibits interference with these means, as well as deliberate concealment measures. To enhance verification, it includes detailed definitions of limited systems and establishes limits on the testing of MIRVed launchers. Finally, a framework was established for the SCC to promote the objectives and implement the provisions of the treaty.

History of Compliance

As a consequence of the 1979 Soviet invasion of Afghanistan, the Carter Administration requested the Senate to suspend proceedings for the ratification of the treaty. The Reagan Administration opposes Senate ratification on the grounds that SALT II is "fatally flawed." President Reagan has attempted to pursue new strategic arms reduction talks (START) with the Soviet Union. In the meantime, however, the administration has stated that the United States will abide by the provisions of SALT II, as long as the Soviet Union also abides by them. The Soviet Union has made a similar statement.

4 | Containing the Threat of Nuclear Terrorism

Barry M. Blechman

THERE IS AN increasing danger that nuclear weapons may fall eventually into the hands of rogue third nations or even subnational groups. While the risk might appear small at present, it would be short-sighted and imprudent to overlook the possibility that international terrorism might one day acquire a nuclear dimension.

Such an event could have grave effects. The opportunities it would present for attempted political (or even financial) extortion could seriously threaten American interests. The actual detonation of a nuclear device by a terrorist group, depending on its target, could cause unprecedented losses of lives and property. Moreover, if a third party's nuclear weapon were directed against the territory or overseas interests of the United States or the Soviet Union (or one of the other three declared nuclear powers), the consequences might be particularly grave. Aside from the immediate losses of lives and property that would result, any such explosion would bear implicitly a serious danger of catalyzing a U.S.-Soviet nuclear exchange because of an erroneous perception on the part of the target state that, directly or indirectly, the second great nuclear power had been at fault.

These potential risks are serious enough to merit careful evaluation and preparatory actions by the U.S. government. Most of the measures which can help to prepare for these eventualities can be performed unilaterally: contingency planning and scenario gaming, the training and exercise of special military and police units, the allocation of intelligence resources, and the like. In addition, though, it may be possible to reduce the risk of nuclear terrorism through international cooperation, just as it has proved possible at least to slow the proliferation of nuclear weapons to other nations through international cooperation. Moreover, insofar as the Soviet Union has such significant nuclear capabilities and often conflicting interests with the United States, it is particularly important to seek ways to cooperate with the USSR to reduce the risk that nuclear weapons might fall one day into the hands of subnational groups and to contain the dangers should such a contingency nonetheless occur.

The U.S. government could explore the possibility of establishing a new U.S.-Soviet forum and system of communications dedicated to reducing the threat of nuclear terrorism. Each nation could establish a watch center in its capital, manned on a twenty-four hour basis by military officers and experienced diplomats and linked together by sophisticated, real-time communications. Consideration should be given also to the assignment of liaison officers from the second state to each center. These new institutions have been termed "Nuclear Risk Reduction Centers," but the title would be unimportant.

The directors of each center would report directly to senior authorities in the two capitals. The directors would remain in direct contact during crises or periods in which crises seemed to be developing and also would meet periodically in normal times to exchange various sorts of information that could help to avoid such situations. These Nuclear Risk Reduction Centers might help to contain nuclear dangers in a variety of ways, as described in the *Report of the Nunn-Warner Working Group on Nuclear Risk Reduction* (Appendix A) and the article by Richard Betts in this volume, but their primary purpose would be to avert the long-term risks associated with the proliferation of nuclear capabilities to subnational groups.

In proposing that the U.S. government consider negotiating with the Soviet Union to establish means of avoiding contingencies involving the acquisition of nuclear weapons by subnational groups, it is assumed that the mutual interest of the U.S. and the USSR in avoiding nuclear war would make it possible to cooperate in this way despite the many differences and conflicting interests between the two nations. There is substantial evidence to support this viewpoint, as described later. It is assumed further, however, that the exchange of information and other functions made possible by the establishment of Nuclear

Risk Reduction Centers could make a meaningful difference in preventing or containing such incidents, and that these benefits would
outweigh the costs that might also be associated with the creation of
such a forum. This conclusion is more controversial; the case is laid out
in the final section of this article.

CONTINGENCIES

One can construct literally dozens of scenarios in which a nuclear-
armed, irresponsible third nation or subnational group might threaten
international peace and security.

A crude nuclear device might be fabricated covertly by an irresponsible state then presumed not to have a nuclear capability, or even by a
terrorist group. The possibility of this happening without the knowledge of the great powers' intelligence agencies is small, but will increase over the years as more individuals study nuclear physics and
engineering and as the know-how, equipment, and materials necessary
to build nuclear weapons continue to proliferate around the globe. The
technology of nuclear bombs is nearly 40 years old; it no longer
represents the forefront of technological know-how. Moreover, there
are intrinsic and unavoidable links between civilian nuclear power
programs and the capabilities necessary to build nuclear weapons.
Although systems of international safeguards can reduce, and already
have reduced, the risk that components and materials intended for
peaceful civilian purposes might be manipulated covertly for weapon
programs, a foolproof system has yet to be, and probably never will
be, devised.

Even so, a more realistic way for a subnational group, at least, to
obtain a nuclear weapon would be to acquire it surreptitiously from the
arsenal of an existing nuclear power. There have been many reports,
for example, of Libya attempting to do just that — both by dealing
directly with the government of a nuclear state (China in one case) and
by attempting to suborn individuals conceivably in a position to facilitate the unauthorized acquisition of a nuclear device. A terrorist organization also might attempt to steal one or more nuclear weapons from
an existing arsenal without the complicity of individuals in official
capacities.

While it appears that the controls on U.S. nuclear weapon stocks are
adequate to minimize the risk of any such contingency, there is little

information available about the control procedures practiced by other nuclear powers. This type of threat may increase in the future, moreover, as additional nations acquire nuclear capabilities. There were substantial problems with the security of American nuclear weapons deployed abroad as late as the early 1970s, twenty-five years after the United States had first manufactured such devices; it would not be exceptional if new nuclear powers took many years to develop sophisticated command and control procedures as well.

Looking toward the future, there also may be reason for concern that one or more nuclear-armed nations might help subnational groups to acquire nuclear weapons. There are past examples of nuclear powers helping other nations to develop nuclear arms — most recently, China has been reported to have provided nuclear weapon design information to Pakistan. And there also are many contemporary examples of national governments aiding terrorist organizations to acquire military equipment, training, and munitions. Although one might think that calculations of self-interest would deter states from aiding subnational groups in acquiring nuclear capabilities, the excesses of recent history would suggest that such rational calculations carry little weight in some regions of the globe.

Once nuclear weapons were in the hands of subnational organizations or irresponsible national leaders, the opportunities for mischief could be endless; many imaginative possibilities have already been detailed in popular books and movies. We need not repeat the many possible forms of coercion or actual military actions which would become feasible. Suffice it to note one particularly disturbing possibility.

Consider the risks associated with the detonation of a nuclear device by a subnational group against a unit of the armed forces of one of the great powers deployed overseas. Imagine, for example, a situation like that which obtained in the Middle East in 1973. The armies of Israel and several bordering Arab nations had been locked in combat in a rapidly changing tactical situation. The United States and the Soviet Union had deployed substantial naval and air forces to the region and had made threats against one another and against the belligerents. If, at the height of this confrontation, a nuclear weapon had exploded on or near a naval unit of one of the great powers, the danger of a U.S.-Soviet nuclear conflict could have been very substantial. The party responsible for the explosion might well have been uncertain; the other great power, one of the local belligerents, or a subnational group concerned with the regional situation all could conceivably have been to blame. Depending on the specific circumstance of the explosion and available intelligence information, the actions of the state whose forces had been victimized by the nuclear blast could easily lead to further escalation. In short, the situation would be uncertain and unstable; the upper bound on the potential violence before its effective resolution would not be obvious at all. It is this type of dangerous situation which Nuclear Risk Reduction Centers would most importantly seek to avoid or, failing that, to contain.

PRECEDENTS

The United States and the Soviet Union clearly recognize both the dangers associated with the spread of nuclear weapons and the risks of accidental and catalytic nuclear war. In their common efforts to contain these dangers, the two great powers have exhibited an unusual willingness and ability to cooperate with one another. A complete catalog of treaties and other agreements which provide precedents for the establishment of nuclear risk reduction centers is presented by William Lynn elsewhere in this volume. In this section, I highlight the most important of these illustrations of previous cooperative actions.

U.S.-Soviet cooperation to stem nuclear proliferation resulted in the 1968 Non-Proliferation Treaty and the safeguards administered by the International Atomic Energy Agency which are designed to ensure compliance with the limitations contained in that treaty. Less publicly, and perhaps more effectively, U.S.-Soviet cooperation made possible the creation of the so-called London Suppliers' Club, in which the nations which manufacture equipment that could be used for the production of materials and components necessary for the fabrication of nuclear weapons have exchanged sensitive information and agreed to prohibit sales of certain types of equipment to nations believed to be seeking nuclear weapon capabilities. While none of these mechanisms have proved to be fully effective, most observers would agree that the proliferation of nuclear weapon capabilities has proceeded at a far slower pace than might have occurred in their absence.

There also are precedents for bilateral U.S.-Soviet actions dedicated to reducing the risk of nuclear conflicts. As early as 1963, the two nations indicated their common recognition of the danger of nuclear war by agreeing to establish direct communications between their two capitals — the so-called hot line. Subsequent agreements in 1971 and 1984 improved the hot line by replacing its original land-lines with satellite links and by adding a facsimile transmission channel to the original teletype system. The Soviet Union also has established direct, dedicated communications links with London and Paris.

In 1971, the United States and the USSR concluded an Agreement to Reduce the Risk of Outbreak of Nuclear War. In this treaty, inter alia, the two nations committed themselves:

> To maintain and to improve . . . organizational and technical arrangements to guard against the accidental or unauthorized use of nuclear weapons;
> To notify each other immediately in the event of an accidental, un-authorized, or any other unexplained incident involving a possible detonation of a nuclear weapon which could create a risk of outbreak of nuclear war;
> To hold consultations . . . to consider questions relating to implementation of the provisions of this agreement.

Pursuant to the final obligation just listed, specific message formats and other measures have been worked out to implement the provisions of the Accidents Agreement. The existing agreement does not call for the establishment of a permanent forum to discuss these issues. Nor does it deal with the danger of nuclear detonations by third parties. Both aspects would follow naturally from the existing agreement, however, and would represent useful extensions of this first, limited attempt to deal with the potential problem of inadvertent nuclear war.

There already exists, of course, a permanent forum to discuss certain nuclear issues—the Standing Consultative Commission (SCC) established by the 1972 ABM Treaty and the Interim Agreement on Offensive Weapons concluded in that same year. While not dealing directly with the issues of accidental or catalytic nuclear wars, the SCC in many ways provides important precedents for the proposed Nuclear Risk Reduction Centers.

The SCC is charged with considering questions of compliance with the obligations contained in the two agreements already mentioned. In support of that purpose, the two parties committed themselves to provide information (on a voluntary basis) necessary to ensure confidence in compliance and to consider other factors bearing on the objectives and implementation of the treaties.

In practice, the SCC has developed into a low-key, professional, and largely confidential forum. For the most part, politics and political disputes have been kept out of its sessions. And, by most accounts, the scc has worked well for more than ten years, during a period of rapid change and considerable strain in U.S.-Soviet relations.

Obviously, the Soviet Union perceives advantage in its participation in these forums that extends beyond their implications for the risk of nuclear war. In a sense, the linkage of the United States and the Soviet Union in these special bodies, for which participation is reserved for the great powers and the great powers alone, helps to legitimate the USSR as the equal of the United States. Symbolically, at least, they have an adverse effect on U.S. interests by putting distance between ourselves and our allies and by linking us, in the eyes of the world, with the Soviet Union. Bodies like the scc give credence to charges often heard in the third world that the United States and the Soviet Union cooperate to the detriment of others; that the great powers tacitly observe certain rules so that, together, they may each benefit at the expense of others. Without exaggerating the importance of such perceptions, it is the case that they do constitute an adverse consequence of the creation of bilateral U.S.-Soviet forums.

The creation of a new forum to exchange information on, and to take other actions about, third-party nuclear threats could be expected to have similar effects, heightened, perhaps, by the sensitive nature of the new forum's proposed subject matter. This is a risk to be weighed. It may be possible to deal with the dangers of third-party nuclear weapons on an ad hoc basis, as they arise. In 1977, for example, when it appeared that South Africa was about to detonate a nuclear device, the United States and the USSR cooperated to help avert that incident — cooperation which included the exchange of sensitive information and actions taken vis-à-vis third parties. The question which must be evaluated is whether the advantages of a regular forum for discussions and the exchange of information on these subjects prior to an actual incident, as compared to ad hoc forms of cooperation, exceed the political disadvantages of creating a new U.S.-Soviet forum.

Mechanisms and Modalities

The establishment of Nuclear Risk Reduction Centers would facilitate the periodic and timely exchange of information that could contribute to averting the threat of nuclear terrorism. The existence of these centers would establish and legitimize the bureaucratic organizations and patterns of interaction necessary for governments to carry out such functions effectively on a regular basis. It would permit some joint planning for certain contingencies to be carried out and provide opportunities for the two great powers to think through the various problems which might emerge in the future. While there would be no guarantee of success in any of the activities described in this section, the extraordinary risks associated with the threats, which conceivably might come into being, suggest that all possible efforts be made to limit future dangers.

The types of information which might be exchanged by the staffs of the two centers and the other activities which they might carry out require careful study. Sensitive data and sources of information would have to be protected. Both sides would want to protect themselves also against the risks of disinformation and deception. In view of the suspicions that exist between the two nations, it is clear that any exchange of information would have to begin at a fairly superficial level, expanding only slowly in scope and intensity if mutual confidence developed between the two sides.

Potential functions that might be considered for the Nuclear Risk Reduction Centers are described in the following text.

1. *Joint planning for nuclear terrorism.* The proposed centers could be used to develop procedures that might be followed in the event of various contingencies. Among the possibilities which could be discussed would be threats by groups claiming to have access to nuclear weapons, unexplained nuclear explosions, and the discovery that nuclear weapons or materials were missing from a nuclear power's stockpile. Plausible scenarios could be discussed, all in a theoretical way, and possible ways to deal with the situation evaluated from the two sides' perspectives. Particular attention might be paid to mechanisms for assuring one another that the other was not at fault, and to means of sharing intelligence information without compromising sensitive sources. Thought might be given to the use of simulations and gaming in order to gain mutual understanding of the types of actions that would be most helpful in the event of various contingencies, and also to identify those actions that would be counterproductive.

The purpose of these planning exercises would not be to reach any sort of agreement on specific procedures to be followed in specific contingencies. The range of plausible scenarios and circumstances is far too broad to detail what should be done in any specific case. Besides, neither nation would be willing to commit itself to specific actions in some future situation whose details and surrounding circumstances cannot possibly be known in advance. Rather, the purpose would be to develop a common understanding of the problems that could be confronted and the types of activities that would be most important and helpful if such an event actually occurred. The development of such routines, such "scripts" for future actions, could help to eliminate missteps if the contingencies ever came into being.

2. *Exchanging information about nuclear safety devices and safeguards.* It is in the mutual interest of the United States and the Soviet Union that they each deploy the most advanced and effective safeguards on their nuclear weapons, to include both devices to prevent such weapons from falling into the hands of unauthorized personnel and those to prevent the detonation of such weapons when not specifically sanctioned by the highest national authorities. Exchanges of information about these safety devices and safeguards would necessarily be tightly circumscribed by the need to avoid compromising weapon design parameters or other critical technologies or military procedures; still, discussions about such technologies in general terms might prove to be of some benefit. The two states also may find it mutually beneficial to transfer information about effective safety and control mechanisms to smaller nuclear powers, in which case less than state-of-the-art information might prove useful. This argues for expanding the forum at times to include other nuclear weapon states.

3. *Exchanging information about relevant activities of subnational groups.* Each of the great powers can be assumed to possess considerable information about the plans and activities of many subnational groups. Some of this information may overlap; much probably does not. Should intelligence sources reveal a serious effort by a group to acquire nuclear weapons, whether by theft or fabrication, in most circumstances it would be in the interest of the great power acquiring the information to share it with the other great power and to cooperate in thwarting the planned operation. Neither would gain from the possession of nuclear weapons by irresponsible organizations. If the target of the terrorist operation were believed not to be the other great power, but rather a third nuclear power, it might still be beneficial to exchange information in the Risk Centers so as to build confidence in the forum and to ensure cooperation in defeating the attempt to acquire the

nuclear device. Exchanges of this type of information might be limited by fears of compromising sensitive intelligence sources; in most cases, however, it should be possible to reveal the prospective incident without revealing the source of the information.

4. *Notification of missing weapons or nuclear materials*. If one of the great powers determined that one of its weapons had been stolen, or simply was unaccounted for, or if it could not account for a substantial quantity of weapons–grade fissile material, it could help to avoid future problems by informing the other great power of that fact. For one thing, the second great power might be in a position to help locate the weapon or material. For a second, if the group which had obtained the weapon sought to catalyze a U.S.-Soviet conflict, the preemptive exchange of information could help to defeat such an effort.

This type of information exchange could be tricky, however. In the event of a missing nuclear weapon, the nation suffering the loss would probably seek to avoid publicity and might also wish to avoid informing the other nation for fear that the latter could locate and seize the weapon itself in order to examine it. There also would be the danger of a fabricated incident for purposes of disinformation or to test the other's intelligence system. All in all, careful study would have to be made of the circumstances under which this type of exchange might make sense and those under which it could prove counterproductive.

5. *Cooperation in the event of a detonation*. If a third party actually detonated a nuclear device, as in the scenario described earlier in this article, each great power may wish to demonstrate to the other that it was not the responsible party, and that it understood that the other was not responsible either. Steps taken toward this end would likely include the exchange of information at the highest level of government and between local military commanders, and also the movement of military forces and other physical measures to reassure each side that hostile actions were not intended. The hot line, diplomatic channels, and new communications channels between defense ministries proposed by President Reagan in 1984 could be essential in such contingencies. In addition, however, the proposed Nuclear Risk Reduction Centers could be used to amplify the messages passed through these higher-level links and to work out in detail the types of activities which could best allay each side's concerns. Particularly if the Centers had existed and operated effectively for some time before the incident, they might prove especially helpful in dispelling the suspicions that

inevitably would accompany virtually any explosion of a nuclear device.

6. *Cooperation in the event of nuclear threats.* Finally, the proposed centers could be used to work out the details of cooperative U.S.-Soviet ventures in the event of nuclear threats by subnational groups. Representatives of the two states could exchange information about the incident, discuss means of dealing with the threat, and work out the details of any joint operations that might be relevant. Here, again, a history of productive exchanges between the staffs of the Nuclear Risk Reduction Centers would facilitate effective cooperation in the event of crisis.

CONCLUSIONS

It should be evident from the preceding discussion that the proposed Nuclear Risk Reduction Centers would serve largely in preventive roles. If established, the Centers would be intended to make possible the frequent and routine exchange of information between U.S. and Soviet representatives with the aim of preventing incidents involving nuclear threats from, or actual detonations by, third parties and of containing the effects of such events should they occur nonetheless. Exchanges of information about nuclear safety devices and safeguards and about the activities of subnational groups conceivably could help to prevent such incidents from ever taking place. The notification of missing weapons and, most importantly, the development of contingency plans and the prior simulation of various kinds of plausible situations could help to avoid escalation from a single nuclear detonation to a U.S.-Soviet exchange. The existence of the centers would facilitate the exchange of information of mutual benefit in normal times — before a crisis developed. The fact of the centers would make feasible far more effective cooperation should various contingencies actually occur.

The proposed centers should be seen as complements to, not substitutes for, existing communications channels. In the event of contingencies described in this article, direct communications between heads-of-state via the hot line would be essential. So, too, would the far-ranging discussions that are only possible in normal diplomatic channels. In certain circumstances, direct talks between military commanders also would be desirable — a factor which argues for the establishment of a direct military communications channel. The Nuclear Risk Reduction Centers would provide an additional dedicated forum to think through possible situations before they occurred, however, to exchange information that might limit the risk of such situations, and to work out the many details of operations that might become essential to contain such crises should they occur. They would provide a forum to encourage cooperative actions that does not currently exist.

There would of course be costs involved in establishing these centers. Politically, establishment of this new bilateral U.S.-Soviet forum would have the adverse effect, previously mentioned, of linking the United States and the Soviet Union in a way that might be interpreted as concrete evidence of "superpower condominium." The Chinese, particularly, might view the establishment of the centers with suspicion, believing that they were designed largely to contain their own nuclear forces. Additionally, depending on what else were happening in U.S.-Soviet relations, the establishment of Nuclear Risk Reduction Centers could be seen to undercut U.S. efforts to isolate and put pressure on the Soviet Union. On the other hand, the European allies could be expected to look favorably at the establishment of the centers, seeing them as an indicator of a healthy U.S. concern about the risks of nuclear war and thus as a positive step with good effects on overall U.S.-European relations. The initiative also could contribute to broader efforts to improve U.S.-Soviet relations.

Militarily, there would be some risk of compromising sensitive information, or that Soviet representatives might take advantage of the exchanges of information at the centers for disinformation purposes. Still, since all information would be tabled only on a voluntary basis, and since U.S. agencies could be expected to scrutinize any information tabled by the Soviets very carefully, these dangers should not be too severe. Moreover, to the degree the Nuclear Risk Reduction Centers served the purposes for which they had been established, they could ease certain types of potential military threats to U.S. interests (i.e., those posed by subnational groups with nuclear weapons) and also greatly reduce the dangers implicit in the types of scenarios which the centers were established to contend with.

All in all, the establishment of Nuclear Risk Reduction Centers could be very much in the interest of the United States. The administration should think seriously about the idea and to evaluate carefully its advantages and disadvantages. In some presently unknown — even unimaginable — contingency in the twenty-first century, citizens of both the United States and the Soviet Union may be very grateful that their leaders had the foresight to establish a forum to deal effectively with the variety of dangers in the nuclear age.

5 | A Joint Nuclear Risk Control Center

Richard K. Betts

THE PROBLEM AND THE PROPOSAL

War can result from a number of causes. The fundamental one is usually an irreconcilable conflict of interest, but misperception and miscalculation can be contributing causes or "accidental" precipitants of a war that neither side wants. In the nuclear age the United States and the Soviet Union have overwhelming reasons to decide that no dispute is irreconcilable because the costs of total war would dwarf any interest at stake. More than at any previous point in history the superpowers need to worry about the accidental factors in conflict. These could evolve from faulty assessments of a threat posed by the other side (assessments that could encourage preemption) or from precautionary military actions that could in turn be misread by the other side, provoking it to preempt. In a crisis — when nerves are frayed, suspicions are heightened, and time for decision is compressed — the chances increase that miscalculation will produce an escalatory cycle of reactions. The technical conditions encouraging this possibility are also increased to the degree that both sides believe an appreciable portion of their forces is vulnerable to a first strike — and leaders in both the United States and the USSR are likely to maintain this view for some time to come. This assessment places a high premium not only on managing crises but on preventing them.

Of course evaluating the dangers is the task of policy and diplomacy in general. Preventing misunderstanding of particular actions that

65

could aggravate a source of tension, however, may involve more technical matters — for example, interpreting military alerts and communicating concerns associated with them, or credibly explaining actions that the other side might see as a signal unintended by the initiating party. Moreover, the potential for incorrect estimation of threats flows in part from the complexity and asymmetry of normal strategic postures and doctrines, so continuing exchanges aimed at clarifying these factors could reduce the odds of miscalculation in a situation of tension at a later date.

Institutionalizing Consultation

The importance of regular consultation to avoid accidents from more technical factors becomes more acute as fundamental sources of conflict grow, increasing the chances of crisis. Such a situation occurred in the early 1980s, as United States–Soviet relations deteriorated dramatically. In such times of tension, however, arranging special consultations becomes extraordinarily difficult. Suspicion, shrill propaganda, and unilateral moves tend to supersede frank discussions, and exchanges outside normal diplomatic channels decline. (This problem was most dramatically exemplified by Moscow's suspension of arms control negotiations at the end of 1983.) Given this paradoxical combination of the importance of communication and the practical barriers against it, there is particular value in *institutionalized* mechanisms for continuous discussion at the working level, mechanisms that might not be so much at the mercy of political winds as visible exchanges at higher levels.

Finally, there is another potential source of accidental war that could be as significant as misunderstanding of the other superpower, one that could also provide an incentive for further institutionalizing consultation to help override resistance due to the brittle relations between Moscow and Washington. It is the danger of catalytic conflict from actions of third parties, such as terrorists or reckless client states. In this respect nuclear proliferation could present the greatest risk of unintended engagement between the superpowers. The nuclear proliferation issue is one of the few on which the United States and the Soviet Union share strong common interests, and on which cooperation has proved feasible and effective (for example, collaboration in the London suppliers group on restricting the transfer of sensitive nuclear technologies and equipment). Linking a new consultative mechanism to the prevention of catalytic confrontation should be attractive enough to modify or sidetrack objections based on normal reluctance to get involved in exchanging security data with principal adversaries.

A New Mechanism

A Joint Nuclear Risk Control Center would make discussions of ways of dealing with potential accidents a permanent and continuous enterprise. It would supplement other means that are not primarily geared to this function. The hot line is an emergency channel to deal with critical events in progress or on the verge of occurrence. The Standing Consultative Commission (scc) revolves around compliance with arms control agreements and meets only periodically or under special circumstances. A new center, in contrast, would aim at anticipating problems in a broader context and avoiding them through prior understandings.

The center would be a bilateral forum for the superpowers. For the United States especially there would be a need to consult allies and keep them fully informed, but attempting to integrate them into the center would vitiate its effectiveness. Speed, efficiency, and frankness decline in direct relation to the number of parties involved in any discussion all the more so when different sovereign states (rather than just agencies within an individual government) are involved. Issues between the superpowers are complex enough and progress in exchange could only be further complicated by introducing intra-allied disagreements directly — not to mention the problems that including interested major parties, such as China, would raise. Broadening national representation in the center would have symbolic value at best, but genuine multilateralism would ruin it. (The problem is reflected in the fate of the United Nations Military Staff Committee, which "has not deliberated on any substantive matter in 35 years."[1]) Restricting membership need not raise delicate diplomatic issues with American allies — side consultations in the bilateral Strategic Arms Limitation Talks provide satisfactory precedent.

To function effectively, the center should be conceived as one entity with two locations. This situation might appear awkward at first glance but could be resolved by having permanent low-level staff maintain two offices — one site in each capital, linked by teleconferencing — while higher-level commissioners would meet periodically at alternate sites. This system would provide easier interactions between center personnel and the backstopping bureaucracies, which would be lost if the organization had its headquarters in a single neutral site such as Geneva. If either of the two governments was reticent about jumping into a fully collaborative pair of organizations, the two sites of the center could begin as nationally manned units, with a very few liaison officers from the other side. If this arrangement worked satisfactorily, the site offices could be expanded into fully joint manning in both capitals.[2]

More detailed discussion of the center's structure and operation will follow later. First, however, let us consider the specific aims of the organization.

PURPOSES AND FUNCTIONS

The center would seek to help prevent crises, lay groundwork for the more common understandings about potential threats to technical stability, and cooperate against dangerous third-party actions. In principle its work could involve exchanges of data, discussions of particular issues in force posture and doctrine, and consideration of problematic scenarios and possible joint actions. In practice, that is a tall order, since tension, suspicion, and bureaucratic and political conservatism all present obstacles to free and easy discussion of sensitive matters. Thus a prime interest is to preserve as much flexibility as possible in the conception of the enterprise. Flexibility would help avoid requiring such specific commitments in advance that leaders would be reluctant to endorse the concept; it would leave room for evolution and adaptation as circumstances permitted; and it would facilitate any of the specific activities that did get under way. The important drawbacks, risks, or barriers are discussed in the "Risks and Implications" section of this chapter. What follows is an elaboration of the aims in principle, holding the risks in abeyance.

Crisis Prevention

The best way to deal with a crisis is to stop it from happening, and that would be the primary purpose of the new organization. In one sense it would function as a cooperative watch center; that is, monitoring actual sources of conflict at a nascent stage, when explanation or consultation might help nip them in the bud. Additionally, in "normal" times, discussions could seek to anticipate hypothetical problems before they eventuate — especially potential sequences of escalatory precautions in which both sides believe themselves to be acting defensively and prudently while viewing the other as acting provocatively — and consider what measures might avert or ameliorate confrontation. In both cases, the center would provide data to clarify either side's reason for alarm about the other's action or to explain why one's own action should not be construed as threatening. Even if exchanges did not solve the disputes at issue, they might at least increase the stock of mutual understanding of what each side considers threatening and the measures it considers necessary for hedging against threats during crises. Moreover, they might help to clarify what actions are reactive; in the heat of controversy precautionary reactions may easily be misread as initiatives.

At best such consultations might provide some basis — however limited or tentative — for tacit agreements on avoiding certain types of alerts or movements under given circumstances, or for unilateral revisions of standard operating procedures to prevent unintended provocation. For example, consider a situation in which one side had scheduled military maneuvers that coincided with the outbreak of a crisis, and the other side interpreted the action as purposely connected with the crisis and responded with an alert, which the first side then interpreted as an initiative requiring response. The problem would be aggravated to the extent that standard operating procedures (or deliberate decision due to misinterpretation) made the second side's action appear disproportionate to the first's — for example, alerting nuclear components in addition to conventional forces — and thus less perceptibly a reaction to the original maneuver. In theory this situation might be akin to the U.S. DEFCON 3 alert in October 1973, except that the Soviet action provoking it — alerting several airborne divisions — would be part of a previously planned exercise. Even if discussions in the center only helped to make leaders more sensitive to monitoring and intervening in peacetime activities of their own armed services, they would be a useful contribution.

Although problems to be discussed subsequently might present difficulties, it might be worthwhile to discuss certain operational "rules of the game" for alerts, maneuvers, or reinforcements in peacetime that could occasion escalation. In a sense the considerations involved would be analogous to those in the 1972 Incidents at Sea Agreement. That accord provided for notification of naval actions that could endanger navigation or aircraft in flight and barred harassment or close approach to ships. Certain provisions for notification of ground force maneuvers already exist as the result of negotiations on Europe; the center could be a forum for exploring refinements of them, or ways to extend them to other regions. Discussions might more directly focus on applications to nuclear forces. An ambitious possibility would be discussions of limitations on simultaneous nuclear alerts: for example, agreement that partial alert by one side would be followed by proportionately partial alert by the other, rather than full alerts that push crisis escalation higher.[3]

Center discussions could also identify categories of data about forces or procedures that would give the side monitoring questionable activities more confidence in its judgments about what danger they pose: for instance, more certainty about whether exercises of tactical nuclear forces included warheads as well as launchers, or what types of command and control safeguards (such as permissive action links) apply to given forces.

Exchanges might distinguish between two levels of concern for confidence building: "normal" times, and times of growing tension. The former could focus on such things as prior notification of missile tests or large-scale bomber launches, or data exchanges on force structure and posture. The latter would focus more on means for prompt and credible explanations of military activities that increase immediate capability, such as redeployment and reinforcement.

An additional function could be staff consultations on background issues that are pertinent to avoiding or resolving crises but that involve nonobservable factors. They would include primarily issues of strategic doctrine, concepts of stability, linkages between technical aspects of force structure and crisis stability, and the ambiguities of connection between declaratory policy and action policy on these matters. In the United States a critical debate in the past decade involved whether the Soviet Union was committed to a first-strike "war-fighting" nuclear doctrine or whether it accepted the principle of "mutual assured destruction" (MAD) and the unthinkability of using nuclear forces in any capacity other than retaliation. Similarly, Soviet critics charge that U.S. official rhetoric about MAD covered ongoing attempts to maximize first-strike options. These subjects are problematic because much of what they involve is vague, theoretical, tentative, or the subject of some debate or confusion *within* the establishments of both sides. In terms of the potential for miscalculation or misunderstanding, however, these subjects could be most important.

Discussions on such matters would probably have some of the qualities of a bull session, so the center forum could be more conducive to them than would others (such as arms control talks), where official negotiated accords are expected to result or where legal matters of compliance with specific obligations are at issue (such as the SCC). The benefit would be that exchanges on controversial or subjective matters where explicit agreement is unlikely could produce marginal increases in sensitivity or tentative understanding, without disappointing the larger expectations that go with formal negotiations.

Finally, the center could be a place to raise issues of compliance with arms control agreements not covered by the SCC, such as the charges of Soviet violation of biological warfare agreements in the Sverdlovsk incident. Although this function would be somewhat unrelated to the center's other responsibilities, it is reasonable on three grounds. First, in the absence of another officially designated regular mechanism for dealing with such matters, the center would be as good a place as any for working-level consultations. Second, since the governing writ of the center should be as permissive and flexible as possible and specific requirements for agreed results should be avoided, the presumption should be that any matter of concern may be raised unless there is a stipulation to the contrary. And third, to keep the center a thriving enterprise, the agenda should be kept as inclusive as possible to avoid long periods of inactivity.

Cooperation against Third-Party Threats

The American and Soviet staffs of the center might exchange intelligence on other countries' or groups' moves toward nuclear proliferation. The clearest precedent for such an exchange is the 1977 case in which the USSR informed Washington and NATO allies of apparent South African preparations for a nuclear test. This sort of cooperation can be useful where the mutuality of superpower interests is clearest (as on proliferation) and where the superpowers have different intelligence collection assets or patterns of coverage. It would be both most vital and most feasible in regard to potential attempts by terrorists or subnational groups to gain access to nuclear material. Cooperation of this sort would be not only uncontroversial and unobjectionable to the overwhelming majority of other governments but quite popular as well. Therefore it might be an ideal mission to establish the rationale for the center, and emphasizing it could be a way to get the enterprise rolling quickly.

The number of cases in which cooperation against national governments would be practical, however, is very limited. South Africa was not a problem because the United States had no interest in warm relations with Pretoria that would compromise its interest in strong-arm tactics against proliferation. But most potential proliferators are closer to Washington than to Moscow. In the case of Argentina, for instance, numerous considerations — such as supporting the endurance of the new democratic regime — would argue for more-discreet unilateral initiatives and against bringing the Soviets into the picture. It is vital to consult in advance about third-party detonations of any sort, however; a study undertaken by General Richard Ellis, former head of the Strategic Air Command, in response to a request by Senator Sam Nunn, concluded that the possibility of third-party action catalyzing a superpower nuclear exchange in some scenarios is alarmingly real.[4]

In regard to the terrorist possibility, the center could be a forum for contingency planning, exchanging information, and maintaining contact during incidents — for example, consultation on means for determining the nature or origin of unexplained or uncertain detonations such as the "South Atlantic flash" of 1979. Contingency planning might involve procedures to be followed in the event of loss or theft of nuclear weapons, plutonium, or uranium from U.S. or Soviet inventories, or disappearance of fissile materials in transit. To deal with the political problems of considering national action, two principles could be used. First, to keep the programs of British and French allies or those of the Chinese out of contention, it could be stipulated that issues of concern would be limited to those states defined as nonnuclear under the terms of the Nuclear Nonproliferation Treaty of 1968. Second, in regard to other countries, the norm could be established that either side is free to raise questions about a given case, but the other side is bound to engage the question only at its own discretion. This provision is consistent with the notion that cooperation is practical only when mutuality of interest is clear and accepted, and that reticence in a particular instance need not be cited as bad faith.

ORGANIZATION AND OPERATION

The structure of the center and the nature of its activities over time would have to be determined in advance, but the prior determination should strike a balance between murkiness (which could confuse or paralyze the start-up of the organization) and rigidity (which could cut off chances in advance for desirable evolution and elaboration). The best compromise might be a writ that stipulated both a minimum set of requirements and the expectation that broader arrangements would be undertaken at the discretion of both sides as experience with center discussions accumulated.

Staff Support for Defusing Crises

The center could not manage crises, because top officials and their own staffs would inevitably take over. Other organs and channels would be the crucial ones for dealing with immediate high-priority conflicts. The center might, however, be able to perform some ancillary or limited support functions, but this role is only a minor one, not the *raison d'être* for the institution. This aspect of the center's function might come into play if, for example, other elements of leadership or bureaucracy in one country noted an apparently minor yet worrisome and ambiguous change in military posture by the other side in the midst of a confrontation — not a massive nuclear alert, but perhaps a curious shifting of some aircraft from one base to another. The center could be a place to ask for explanations when other channels might be overloaded with communications on more urgent matters. If staffs of the center have established reasonable working relationships and are used to interacting with each other in "normal" times and discussing low-order technical questions on which higher officials have not focused, they might be well geared to exploring *tactical*-level options for de-escalation or disengagement. To have the flexibility to do so, though, it would have to be well understood that center personnel did not necessarily speak for their governments and were only authorized to suggest possibilities, and that no suggestion could be taken as a firm offer by the opposing government. One potential problem with this arrangement, in the context of crisis, is that it might be seen as a license to "smoke out" the opponent, creating suspicious or "Alphonse/Gaston" attempts to get the opponent to be forthcoming first. Even if no agreement or solution were suggested by the discussions in the center, they would at least be a basis for increasing information available to other actors in crisis management; center staffs could report whatever their counterparts said, and the crisis managers could take it or leave it as an intelligence input.

Regular Activities

Exchanges should be as frequent as practical in order to maintain the habit of dialogue, yet not so infrequent that it becomes difficult to fill the agenda. Regular meetings should be held (perhaps bimonthly) to avoid making an issue of whether or not to call a meeting, as well as to prevent any public presumption of malfeasance or noncompliance with agreements if a meeting is called. (These points are suggested by previous experience with the Standing Consultative Commission. In parallel with the two-tier approach of permanent staff and higher-level commissioners, the former could maintain regular dialogue while the latter would handle special meetings related to compliance questions or gathering tensions.)

The center's mandate for discussion should be explicit, stated as an order from highest authority (which would increase Soviet representatives' frankness). It should also be broad in principle (to leave maximum room for evolution) but narrow in concrete requirements (to give the experiment a chance to work). Given the mandate in principle (such as "the parties will discuss means to reduce nuclear risks and exchange data appropriate to that task"), the center personnel themselves could work out the specific agenda once the operation got under way.

Normal military secrecy requirements or political desires to maintain flexibility by preserving ambiguity will pose challenging constraints. The Soviets in particular have traditionally been reluctant to reveal more data than necessary for negotiation of official agreements; by the end of the 1970s, though, they were more forthcoming than they had been in earlier years, so the possibility of greater openness cannot be dismissed. Within whatever limits prove feasible there could be periodic exchanges of data on military forces' composition, exercises, or alert procedures. The focus should be on nuclear forces, although enough flexibility to raise other issues should be retained. Monitoring and discussion of conventional force activities can be appropriate because the danger of nuclear accidents or confrontations could grow out of actions at the conventional level.

Other topics are matters pertinent to avoiding or resolving crises that are not covered in arms control agreements or official understandings. Examples include deterrence concepts, operational doctrine, and connections between technical aspects of force structure and crisis stability.

Staffing and Management

The staff of the center should be small because speed and openness of communication decline as the number of people involved grows. Moreover, the agenda might not be big enough to keep a large number constantly employed. So a large staff would not only aggravate bureaucratic redundancy but also raise the danger of incentives to make work for itself in normal times, and thus possibly increase friction by "creating" crises out of insignificant issues. Finally, if the center is to function in a way that offers policymakers something more useful than they already get from other organs, the staff should be of high quality. One way of dispelling the idea that assignment to the center is not "career-enhancing" is to keep the operation "lean and mean."

Combining this goal with the need to keep the center functioning on a day-to-day basis could be done through the two-tier arrangement suggested above. The small permanent staffs could keep channels open and perhaps engage in follow-up exchanges on details concerning matters discussed by the higher-level commissioners, who would meet only periodically. To preserve flexibility there should be provision for temporary augmentation of either permanent or high-level staff, depending on the issues under discussion at specific meetings.

The representation of both sides' various bureaucratic components in the center should be parallel insofar as possible, though differences in the organization of national security structures preclude absolutely identical composition. Parallelism should be greatest in the first tier of high-level commissioners. Among the most important agency representatives there would be those from the military (the Joint Chiefs of Staff and possibly the Strategic Air Command on the U.S. side, the General Staff and Strategic Rocket Forces on the Soviet side), since the danger of accidental engagements can flow from unanticipated consequences of standard operating procedures. (The latter, of course, is not the only major source of nuclear risks, since political crises create the potential for escalation. Dealing with political conflicts of interest and nipping a confrontation in the bud, however, is for high policymakers not the center staff.) For diplomatic as well as sub-stantive reasons the State Department and the Foreign Ministry should be represented, and so might the Office of the Secretary of Defense (OSD) on the U.S. side and some comparable civilian official for the Soviets (although the lack of a Soviet organization comparable to OSD might make that difficult). At the second tier of permanent staff the same units should also be represented. Representation of other com-ponents at this level might be left more to the discretion of either side. For the United States a Sovietologist should be included, to help gauge likely reactions of the opposing delegation. The Arms Control and Disarmament Agency might participate in some noncrisis functions, especially discussion of formal confidence-building measures. Finally, there should be an *ex officio* member from the National Security Council Staff.

Perhaps most important, however, as well as most delicate, would be the representation from the intelligence community. Information security will be a prime concern and a very difficult issue to manage because there is an obvious severe tension between the aims of the center — greater confidence due to more revelation of information — and normal security. The Soviets are also especially sensitive to the possibility of an adversary using talks for intelligence collection, which direct participation of intelligence officials might symbolize if not managed discreetly. Intelligence representatives would have to be available (at least for the United States) to determine whether certain exchanges would endanger "sources and methods." (The SCC handled this problem by assigning a CIA representative the responsibility for sources and methods and a Defense Department representative the responsibility for protecting U.S. information.) Also (though this might have to be done outside the center staff), there should be some declassification contingency planning for crises — prior determination of what sorts of information could be revealed for purposes of prevent-ing Soviet miscalculation. (Waiting until the moment to consider this question would cause long delays at just the time that expeditious communication is most vital.) At the same time the profile of the intelligence community representative(s) should be kept low because of Soviet suspicions of such forums as intelligence-gathering op-erations. This problem is delicate to manage because in one sense the basic idea for the center, in assuming the desirability of less secrecy, *does* promote intelligence collection.[5]

Responsibility, Coordination, and Control

For the United States the center should report directly to the National Security Council rather than through a department. This chain of command has three advantages. First, the center's functions do not fall clearly within the military, political, or analytical provinces; rather they cross-cut them, so none of the most relevant units — State, Defense, or the Director of Central Intelligence — has a clear claim to responsibility. Second, flexibility might be enhanced if the operation is not dominated by foreign service, military, or other departmental bureaucracies. Third, in crises the center would have to contribute to decision speedily or not at all; direct access to the top would help.

In proposing a new organization it is useful to anticipate charges that it may only be a new layer or redundant complicating factor in government. It is true that the center's functions might overlap to some degree those of other òrgans or channels. In normal exchanges for the crisis prevention purpose, center discussions could wind up treading on the territory of the scc or of relevant negotiations themselves (START, INF, MBFR). In crisis management support activities, there might be some potential overlap with the Strategic Warning Staff, the National Intelligence Officer for Warning (NIO/W), and the hot line. In neither case need the redundancy be substantial, and it could certainly be less than is usual in the other areas of the policy process.

In the first case, negotiations (and the scc, which is meant to deal with implementation of agreements) deal with force structure and force levels, while center talks would deal more with force *status* and operations. (In a sense the former deal with "static" matters subject to formal agreement, the latter with "dynamic" issues or with those too uncertain for clear and binding treaties.) There might be some provision, perhaps informal, for merging scc and center discussions on particular cross-cutting issues. Such cooperation could also be an indirect means of linking center talks with negotiating teams without further complicating the negotiations themselves.

It would not be difficult to differentiate functions in the second case, but the question of communications between the units would have to be handled with care. It might be helpful for the NIO/W to know how Soviet representatives in the center are explaining apparently threatening movements; but it would not be advisable to have warning communiqués flowing freely to the center, where chances of unapproved Soviet access are greater. (A counterargument would be that a warning unit's perspectives should not be compromised by official Soviet statements that could be meant to deceive, and that such statements could be compared to "unadulterated" warning reports at higher levels anyway. It is just as sensible to argue, however, that professional warning officers should have a chance to consider and comment on possible disinformation before top decision makers judge it.) The center offices could have secure facilities and communication links to the warning apparatus and White House Situation Room, but with careful procedures to control sharing. Though it is important to be sure that this process is controlled, however, the problem is not crucial because the center would play a minor role at best in crisis management.

Congressional oversight of the center presents both opportunities and problems. The principal opportunity is that it can help short-circuit public misunderstanding due to suspicion by validating administration claims that Moscow has a satisfactory explanation for questionable activities. The principal problem is the Soviet penchant for insisting on the privacy of discussions, which discourages wider participation and publicity. Both potential aspects are illustrated in the history of the scc, where privacy provisions initially inhibited disclosure of reasons for events that some public critics have charged were SALT violations. One option would be to give normal oversight jurisdiction to the intelligence committees (which have a reputation for leaking less than other committees), with provision for informing other relevant committees on matters of particular interest, while encouraging the Soviets to see how occasional revelations can work in their interest.

RISKS AND IMPLICATIONS

In the largest sense the risks posed by the proposed center flow from the essential dilemma of U.S.–Soviet relations. The superpowers have both cooperative and competitive interests; they share the interest in avoiding armed conflict, but they also seek to prevent each other from gaining any advantage in the balance of power. The matters of concern to the Joint Center for Nuclear Risk Reduction lie in the gray area between cooperation and competition because both sides will be alert to the possibility that any measure that is discussed, or any piece of information revealed at the request of the other side, might help that side disproportionately. The goal is to focus on ways to avoid accidental sources of conflict, which should be matters of equal interest. But both sides will recognize that there can be future conflicts of interest where actions or reactions would be purposeful rather than accidents or miscalculations, and they will want to preserve their options. If one side does miscalculate and act in a dangerous manner, the other will want to be free to react rationally but effectively to counter it. Many of the risks in the center's operation result from these ambiguous tradeoffs. The general norm for trying to manage the tradeoffs should be that the center's mission is to discuss and explore, not to decide or make commitments; when discussions do yield agreement at the center level, consideration of more formal commitments can be passed to higher levels of authority.

Political and Diplomatic

The general potential benefit of the center is to reduce the risk of nuclear war. At best that may be done directly by discussion of matters that could lead to agreements on mutual restraints or operational precautions against unintended provocation. The secondary or indirect benefit would be more wide-ranging, detailed, and regular dialogue, which offers possible gains in reduced misunderstanding, increased confidence, better atmospheric background for other contracts, and the symbolic promise of enhanced cooperation of other issues. Reduction of nuclear risks from this indirect benefit would be a matter of marginal or serendipitous spillover effects, but the priority of the nuclear danger makes even the slightest incidental benefits a warrant for the institution. However, there are several negative developments that must be measured against these aims.

Dialogues in some instances could aggravate conflict rather than alleviate it, for instance, by forcing unresolvable issues into the open or highlighting basic differences of strategy that frustrate agreement. This outcome could be more desirable than the "ignorance is bliss" alternative, but it would then make those irritants harder to ignore, or it could enhance the propaganda position of one side. Perhaps the most general example is related to a basic asymmetry in politico-military strategy. Historically the United States relied on escalation as an instrument of policy, to offset perceived Soviet advantages at lower levels of military power or to make a diplomatic signal particularly dramatic.[6] The last prominent instance of this sort was the DEFCON 3 alert in the 1973 Middle East war. Whether or not actions of this sort are wise or a desirable option to maintain, tradition poses obstacles to American agreement to circumscribe them. The Soviets, however, given favorable inequalities in geography and the size of ground forces, have had less strategic or doctrinal incentive to exploit such options in crises near their borders. They might logically propose extension of the nuclear "no first use" principle (which they have declared and the United States has not) to "no first nuclear alert" or some such variant.

Conversely, the United States could cite the mobilization of ground force units in the Soviet Union, say, in the region near the Persian Gulf, as the first step in an escalatory process. But since Soviet forces in normal times are kept at a proportionally lower level of readiness, they could see limited mobilization as a necessary element in precautionary behavior in a crisis and cite it as less dangerous than the alternative of changing the status of nuclear components. In short, what one side views as fundamental to strategic options as opposed to what is a potential source of accident or miscalculation could be the reverse of the combination seen by the other side. If discussions bogged down in such matters, the apparent utility of the center could diminish.

Another possibility is that if incorrect signals are given inadvertently, the other side may see them as attempted deception or bad faith. This problem is not trivial because one's own policy or doctrine is not always understood in the same way even *within* one's own bureaucracy, while the nature of the center's mandate would put a premium on free discussion — which multiplies the chances for errors or inconsistencies to be communicated.

Clarifying U.S. doctrine might also undermine the "uncertainty" component of deterrence. There is a historic tension in U.S. strategy between acceptance of *mutual* nuclear deterrence and commitment to first use of nuclear weapons to stave off defeat in a European war. Most analysts believe that the second lacks credibility on rational grounds but retains some credibility as long as the Soviets cannot be certain that U.S. leaders accept such a conclusion. Detailed, frank discussions might erode the benign aspect of confusion that underwrites such uncertainty.

Beyond the general value of dialogue another benefit would be the possibility of fostering more consensus on the conceptual frame of reference for mutual interests, particularly in regard to technical norms of stability. There are probably no notable risks attached to this goal.

One possibility that might be considered, however, is that if the Soviets *reject* particular U.S. rationales for finding certain activities threatening, then the United States might be less inclined to respond to such activities if they occur. Or if we did respond, the Soviets could more easily charge that there was no legitimate excuse for the U.S. action, since they had clearly demonstrated why their own action was unobjectionable.

The center's effects on third parties could be both negative and positive. It should help reassure U.S. allies, especially Western European publics, against fears of American nuclear adventurism. It might also marginally enhance joint U.S. and Soviet diplomatic pressures against nuclear proliferation by increasing the credibility of superpower efforts to reduce their own reliance on nuclear weapons. On the other hand, the same efforts could have negative results: by raising European governments' doubts about U.S. commitment to extended deterrence and nuclear first use, by encouraging European and Chinese suspicions about superpower condominium (especially if consultations involved sharing data on British, French, and Chinese strategic forces), or by promoting further Sino–Soviet détente (though that would not be altogether a bad thing). The condominium issue could be especially sensitive, since if the center yields optimum results it could indeed increase the image of a joint security regime being imposed over allies, possibly at their expense. There were murmurings of at least tentative concern on this score from NATO allies in some phases of past arms control negotiations. In most recent times, however, U.S. allies have appeared most concerned about the opposite danger — that the dying of détente between the superpowers threatens them. Therefore, if the center were to get off the ground in the near future, it would almost certainly be welcomed by European NATO members. The condominium issue might only arise in "better times," that is, if the aims of the center — reducing the risk of nuclear war — appear to be achieved to a significant degree. Some of these problems are inevitable, given our NATO allies' traditional alternation between fears that the United States is not sufficiently dependable and fears that it is excessively dependable (that is, provocative). Suspicions might be calmed by keeping allied governments regularly briefed on the talks and soliciting their recommendations for questions to be pursued.

Finally, there is the question of domestic political implications. A positive result might be some calming influence on the U.S. antinuclear movement, and thus some reduction in opposition to weapons modernization programs. The negative risk is that apparent success of center exchanges might exert some lulling effect, highlighting optimistic assumptions and reinforcing skepticism about threat assessments. If secrecy is maximized (as Moscow might wish) domestic impact — whether favorable or not — would be minimized.

Military and Intelligence

Management would be most difficult in the military and intelligence area. At worst the center would not function well and there would be few exchanges that reveal information or ideas in a more useful way than other channels do. That would represent failure but would not introduce new risks into the relationship. It is only if the center *succeeds* in its mission of sharing data or views that are not fully detectable or understandable by "national technical means" that the double-edged quality of some of its activities could be problematic. Voluntary revelation of information can reassure an opponent, but to the extent that such reassurance depends on trust it can be an occasion for deception or manipulation. In creating reciprocal obligations, exchange can also pose problems for preservation of one's own information security and operational flexibility.

For intelligence collection and analysis, the most positive result would be to increase the amount of available data and official Soviet signals about doctrine and operational concerns. The negative possibilities would be a compromise of our military plans or intelligence assets, increased vulnerabilities to deception, or a temptation to accept unequal exchanges of data (since the Soviets have been traditionally less willing to see benefits in transparency). A related criticism might be that overanxiousness to maintain dialogue might increase the chances of revealing too much or enhancing the understanding of matters better left misunderstood. For example, better information on the opponent's force structure and procedures could overlap with the information that is useful for offensive targeting. With careful prior planning, however, there is no reason for that to occur — stalling the talks would be more likely than foolish breaches of secrecy.

The greatest overall risk associated with center activity is its vulnerability to Soviet disinformation (possible compromise of sensitive U.S. information is another danger to guard against, but that is within U.S. control). If exchanges in the center are to be an improvement over what is offered by mechanisms already in place, both sides will have to be forthcoming. On many issues there may be no way to assure the Soviets' veracity; if all their explanations could be reliably checked by independent means, there would be less need for this mechanism in the first place. Perhaps a team of devil's advocates — making a case for the reasons a given Soviet explanation might be questioned or rejected — should be integrated in the operation, if not in the center itself then in the backstopping apparatus.

In dealing with the potential for accidental engagement of military forces the potential benefits of the center might be to reduce the chances by clarifying potentially dangerous circumstances, reaching tacit agreements on avoiding such circumstances, or expanding or refining the 1971 Accidents Measures Agreement. The negative outcome, as with many confidence-building measures (CBMs), is that such progress could restrict our own military flexibility. It might, for example, reinforce political pressures against quick response to apparent Soviet war preparations; there might be inhibitions against abrogating CBMs right after Moscow does, lest we blur the issue of who is at fault in the crisis.

The danger of deception is linked to the natural continuing competition for strategic advantage. Ambitious proposals would heighten suspicions that one side was seeking to disarm, delay, or hamper the other's options for legitimate defensive reaction in a crisis by posing those options as dangerous sources of "accidental" escalation. Placing a high premium on avoiding risk of accident may be seen to paralyze initiative or prevent proper precautions. Asymmetries in organizational structure and SOPs also mean that certain hypothetical "brake" mechanisms for crisis prevention or management would affect one side's options more than the other's. Reinforcement of crisis stability through risk reduction could conflict with views that deterrence is sometimes reinforced through deliberate manipulation of risk. Yet the fact remains that both sides do recognize the danger of accident; the problems mentioned may obstruct some agreements but should not preclude discussion. Precedent for revelation of sensitive information when conditions warrant exists in the SCC.[7]

The positive results in regard to nuclear proliferation would be increased chances of leverage against potential proliferators due to increased information available or expanded consultation on measures mutually desired by the superpowers. The risk would be that evidence of "elitist" superpower "collusion" to maintain nuclear duopoly might spur proliferators' incentives. One consideration is whether U.S.–Soviet consultations would be linked to cooperative preventive measures — for example, joint diplomatic initiatives, economic pressure, or other actions.

Conclusion

High expectations that the center would be a major breakthrough of some sort would have to rest on two kinds of extreme optimism — about how many of the elements of the risk of war are only problems of communication and misperception, and about the willingness of either government to maximize the open exchange of information. Ambitious hopes and optimistic assumptions fit best into a dubious conception of East–West relations that sees conflict as the unnecessary product of misunderstanding or unfounded mutual suspicion. Unfortunately the essential conflicts of interest are real, so even the maximum benefits of focusing on sources of miscalculation will be limited. The opposite conception of East–West competition — that it is inevitably unremitting and involves negligible common interests — allows little room to see benefits in a joint center. Thus the rationale for the center that makes most sense, and is not hostage to excessive optimism, rests on the notion of a mixed U.S.–Soviet relationship, in which cooperative avoidance of risk is a shared interest but also in which legitimate suspicions based on competitive interests will limit exchanges or agreements. In this context huge strides in accommodation should not be the standard for success; small steps are worth effort and experimentation. In late 1983 the U.S. and Soviet governments discussed the possibility of establishing something like the center proposed here.[8] Although their ideas about the focus of exchanges differed somewhat, enough common ground existed — despite the heat of relations in general at that point — to suggest optimism.

If the center is established it will only be one of several tools available to the National Security Council, not necessarily "the" one of importance. It will be useful to keep that in mind in order to avoid overselling the center's importance, which could produce disappointment. Along with the scc, however, the center could not only help reduce risks but also supply some continuity of discussions across administrations — and discontinuity has been a problem in arms control. Altogether a Joint Center for Nuclear Risk Reduction would not offer tremendous promise of great breakthroughs in U.S.–Soviet relations, but would offer modest yet possibly meaningful improvements in communication. In a period of somber prospects for superpower relations, modest progress would represent a major achievement.

NOTES

1. William Lynn, "Existing U.S.–Soviet Confidence-Building Measures," chapter 3, this volume.

2. "A Nuclear Risk Reduction System," Appendix A, this volume.

3. On the dangers of simultaneous alert see John Steinbruner, "Nuclear Decapitation," *Foreign Policy* 45 (Winter 1981-82).

4. "A Nuclear Risk Reduction System."

5. Of more than minimal importance is assurance that competent language interpreters are integrated in the organization, including planning sessions. Since on the one hand the sorts of misunderstandings of concern to the center can turn on a nuance, and on the other hand the purpose of the organization is to encourage as much freedom of discussion as possible (as opposed to the more plodding or carefully planned formal proposals characteristic of regular negotiations), it is important to avoid translation mistakes. Therefore, interpreters need to be apprised in advance of what is likely to be said.

6. See Richard K. Betts, "Elusive Equivalence: The Political and Military Meaning of the Nuclear Balance," in Samuel P. Huntington, ed., *The Strategic Imperative* (Cambridge: Ballinger, 1982), pp. 109, 112-117.

7. See Robert W. Bucheim and Dan Caldwell, "The U.S.–USSR Standing Consultative Commission: Description and Appraisal," Working Paper No. 2 (Center for Foreign Policy Development, Brown University, May 1983); and Jane M. O. Sharp, "Confidence Building Measures and SALT," *Arms Control* III, No. 1 (May 1982): 39-42.

8. Charles Mohr, "Talks Urged for Averting Accidental Nuclear War," *New York Times*, November 24, 1983, p. A11; "U.S. and Soviet Seek to Prevent a Surprise Attack," *New York Times*, December 8, 1983, p. A6.

6 | Restrictions on Weapon Tests as Confidence-Building Measures

Sidney D. Drell and Theodore J. Ralston

ONE OF THE most effective elements of successful arms control agreements between the United States and the Soviet Union has been restraints on the testing of new or improved weapons. Focusing on the testing phase of the weapon development process has (1) permitted the achievement of substantial restraint in the development of destabilizing antiballistic missile technologies through the ABM Treaty; (2) retarded the development of destabilizing ballistic missile capabilities, such as increased numbers of reentry vehicles, maneuvering reentry vehicles, fractional orbital bombardment systems, depressed trajectory systems, and more than one new type of ICBM through the SALT II definitions hinged to types of ICBMs *tested;* and (3) permitted an effective verification regime keyed to the most readily verifiable phase of the weapon development cycle, the test phase. While it is frequently observed that an approach to controlling weapons development through restraints on testing promotes greater stability and increases the effectiveness of verification, an additional fundamental point is often overlooked — restrictions on weapon tests can contribute to building confidence necessary to maintain a balance in overall weapons capability. This latter point is a necessary requirement for deterrence. It is our intent to examine how restrictions on testing can build confidence.

OBJECTIVES

In examining this question, we first address the relevant elements of the testing phase of weapons development. Second, we set out the goals and principles underlying the utility of test restrictions as arms control. Third, we suggest the scope and type of restrictions that should be considered and set out the criteria by which to evaluate them. Fourth, we attempt to illustrate the value of flight test restrictions for the case of hard-target, first-strike weapons by showing the effect a reduction in the number of permitted flight tests of ICBMs would have on the military planning requirement for high confidence in performance and reliability.

TEST STAGES

There are two reasons for testing programs. One is to develop new weapon systems and see how well they work. A second and important reason is to increase the performance and reliability of systems already deployed. The development of new systems typically incorporates three test stages. The first is laboratory testing, or what is called "R&D tests" or "design bureau tests."[1] This stage can encompass a relatively broad range of tests, ranging from component or subsystem testing (such as static tests of new rocket motors and tests of new types of arming or fusing devices) to short-range flights of a full system. The second stage, called Initial Operational Test and Evaluation (IOT&E), can include a series of tests performed with early-production models of an aircraft or missile, the purpose of which is to evaluate the components before a commitment is made to full-scale production for deployment. The final stage of testing is called Field Operational Test and Evaluation (FOT&E), in which the purpose is to test the full system as it will be deployed. Anywhere from 5 to 10 percent of the total number of the weapon to be deployed typically are tested in order to achieve a statistically significant number for judging the system's reliability. In the case of aircraft and missiles, the FOT&E group of flight tests is usually followed by occasional tests of operational systems to permit continued confidence in their operational reliability.

In discussing potential negotiated restraints on weapon tests we shall not consider limits on the research or conceptual development work that goes on in the laboratory. Restraints on this phase of testing would be unverifiable — at least without exceedingly intrusive on-site inspection that would undoubtedly be unacceptable to all parties concerned. Furthermore, such restraints would leave each side more uncertain about new technological possibilities than they are currently, and thus increase their respective concern about the possibility of technological breakthroughs. The precedent of distinguishing component and conceptual development work, on the one hand, and field work on prototype systems, on the other, was established in the ABM Treaty of 1972. We shall consider in this paper only the impact of restraints on tests of full prototype systems.

GOALS AND PRINCIPLES

It is important to set out the goals of arms control in order to specify the underlying purposes to which restrictions on testing activity can contribute. It is our view that there are three primary goals of arms control:

1. Improving stability
2. Maintaining deterrence at lower levels of destructive power
3. Saving money

Restrictions on testing can contribute to each of these goals. Stability in the balance of forces can be enhanced through restrictions on the development of weapon capabilities which if deployed would give one side a significant advantage over the other — e.g., a new generation of very accurate missiles with a large number of independently targetable warheads. One logical step is to restrict the development of such capabilities by slowing the rate at which these capabilities are tested, thereby slowing the rate at which they are eventually added to operational forces.

Similarly, restrictions on testing can contribute to maintaining deterrence in several ways. First, depending on the restrictions, the inability to test potentially destabilizing capabilities fully can retard confidence that the weapons will perform reliably or to their full potential. Under such circumstances it is unlikely that prudent military planners would choose to deploy these systems. The effect would be to prevent further addition of greater numbers or greater destructive power to existing force levels. Second, in order for deterrence to work effectively, each side must believe it can respond appropriately and in sufficient time to any new weapons development by the other side.

Testing restrictions that have the effect of stretching out the development time for weapons that are eventually deployed can provide this margin of time.

Lastly, restrictions on testing activity — either in scope, magnitude, or depth — can save money by reducing the extensive field and operational test programs that are an expensive part of the life cycle for deployed weapons. For those weapon capabilities that are ultimately not deployed, more money can be saved by eliminating the field and operational testing altogether.

Confidence-Building Steps

Having stated the broad arms control goals, the principles on which testing restriction agreements would be based need to be set out. The basic question is how to build confidence between two essentially adversarial nations. One way to build confidence is to take steps that would reduce their respective uncertainty concerning the future magnitude, characteristics, and missions of the other side's weapon programs. The United States, for example, was quite uncertain in 1984 about whether then-recent tests of what are reported to be two new Soviet ICBMs portended major changes in Soviet ICBM force posture and characteristics. U.S. uncertainty was further aggravated by the question of whether these tests violated the provisions of the 1979 SALT II Treaty permitting only one new type of ICBM. One can imagine similar uncertainties circulating within the Kremlin with respect to U.S. plans for the MX, "Midgetman," maneuvering reentry vehicles, or supersonic long-range cruise missiles.

Negotiated test restrictions can contribute to confidence-building by aiding assessments as to the purpose and mission of a new system. Provisions restricting the number of tests can reduce concerns about rapid breakout from negotiated restrictions on forces in arms-control treaties by prolonging the time it takes to achieve new operational capabilities. Provisions restricting test practices to only those consistent with an agreed-upon mission can help reduce uncertainty about secondary missions, which might put deterrent forces at risk, in two ways. First, an agreed mission consistent with deterrence would prescribe the permitted "test envelope" — those test performance criteria and specifications appropriate to the mission, deviation from which would clearly signal a different intent. For example, during the SALT II debate concern was frequently expressed in the United States over the possibility that the Soviet *Backfire* bomber might have an intercontinental mission rather than being restricted solely to roles in theater warfare, as claimed by Soviet spokesmen. The inclusion of a provision defining a test performance profile in conjunction with a requirement to declare test ranges could have helped reduce the uncertainties. Were the *Backfire* to be tested in a profile inconsistent with an intermediate-range mission, such a change would be apparent. Second, because a deviation from the agreed mission profile would be evident, uncertainties related to verification would be reduced, contributing to increased confidence.

Another principle for building confidence successfully is a willingness to make fair trades, or balanced and reciprocal concessions in negotiations. This principle recognizes the asymmetries in the two nations' force postures and development processes while at the same time demonstrating a mutual intent toward restraint. The key questions are how to determine what would be equitable as well as what steps would lead to a more stable balance.

The third principle of confidence-building is dependable verification and compliance. This requirement would be relatively easy to satisfy with restraints on testing of systems because its violations in a test program would be readily detectable. Flight tests of missiles or aircraft, in the initial-test or field-test stage, are the most readily verifiable. Lingering doubts about problems associated with systems of variable ranges, such as cruise missiles, which can be tested over relatively short ranges in the interior part of either country, could be diminished by agreement to declare test ranges in advance. This approach would have the advantage of substantially easing the monitoring tasks. Detection and analysis of a new weapons capability that did not involve a full test program would be more difficult than for a full program. However, such a test program would most likely involve a sufficient number of tests at least to raise the level of concern and analytic attention. Further, the value of whatever results were obtained from a shortened test program would have to be weighed against the concomitant decrease in the military reliability and questionable performance of the new system. Again, adoption of an agreed testing profile linked to a mission would help focus and clarify monitoring by specifying expected performance characteristics.

VALUE OF FLIGHT TEST RESTRICTIONS

Several types of restrictions on weapons testing could be equitable, could reduce uncertainty on both sides, and would be verifiable. In the first instance, they are related to flight tests of ballistic and cruise missiles and aircraft. Negotiability is a key factor, and there must be some realistic basis on which to pin negotiations on these restrictions, such as a previous agreement or negotiating track record. Examples of such broad restrictions are the following:

1. Declared times during which tests may be conducted
2. Declared test ranges and facilities
3. Prior notification of test activity
4. Prohibitions on concealment, deception, interference, and denial of data (e.g., encryption), coupled with verification standards regulating the type, quantity, and quality of data to be made available
5. Joint observation of tests

A negotiated requirement to provide notification of launches of more than one missile could reduce the risk of accidental nuclear war, or at least public perception of such risks. Such a provision was agreed to in SALT II for ICBMs and the Soviets even went as far as to announce the dual, simultaneous launch of an ICBM and SLBM after SALT II was signed. The provision in SALT II required an announcement of an impending launch through a "Notice to Mariners" closing a specified missile impact area at sea. The time and place of launch and the coordinates of the impact area had to be provided within the "Notice." A requirement to provide trajectory data would make this step even more reassuring. Such a requirement would make it easier for each side to observe the other's missile tests, thereby increasing their confidence in their assessment of the other's capabilities.

Restrictions on encryption or other means of denying telemetry from missile tests are generally recognized as a necessity for ensuring the verifiability of qualitative restrictions on missiles. What is sometimes overlooked in discussions of this issue, however, is that agreement to prohibit means of denying data reinforces the value each party places in its independent ability to verify compliance. An important degree of confidence derives from this independence because the tools each party uses to verify compliance are under their unilateral control, which reduces the chances that false or misleading data can be introduced into the verification process. Since encryption has no other purpose than to keep the data secret from nonauthorized observers (hence denial), the willingness to prohibit encryption (or at least to restrict it sharply) can be seen as a confidence-building measure. This type of measure also has the advantage of having already once been negotiated in SALT II. A broader agreement, therefore, might also be negotiable.

In addition to these broad provisions, it would be necessary to have certain agreements that pertained only to particular types of weapon systems. One possibility would be "testing type rules" for such "dual capable" weapons as cruise missiles or bombers; these weapon systems can be used for nuclear missions, but also for missions utilizing only conventional ordnance. As with other "type rules," the idea is that after testing of a system in a particular configuration or for a certain mission, that configuration or mission would define the system for the purposes of an agreement, regardless of actual deployment. This is not a perfect solution for verifying compliance with negotiated restrictions, but it does make circumvention somewhat more difficult.

FLIGHT TEST RESTRICTIONS TO IMPROVE THE SURVIVABILITY OF RETALIATORY FORCES

A principal arms control objective is to improve confidence in the survivability of each side's retaliatory force. Improvements in the accuracy of ICBMs can threaten this objective. For example, improved accuracy leads to the ability to further fractionate payload by adding more and smaller reentry vehicles (either overtly or surreptitiously through simulation or extra weight). This would render hardened second-strike forces more vulnerable to a first strike. Testing restraints can help to alleviate this problem.

One possibility is to restrict maneuvers of a missile's postboost vehicle (PBV), the final stage of a missile equipped with multiple independently targetable warheads, which controls, targets, and releases the warheads (called reentry vehicles). An approach that has been successfully negotiated is contained in the Second Agreed Statement to paragraph 10 of Article 4 of the SALT II Treaty, which keys the number of "procedures for releasing" reentry vehicles on any new strategic ballistic missile during flight testing to the maximum number of reentry vehicles on corresponding missile types flight tested before May 1, 1979. This provision defines the "procedures" to mean those maneuvers of the PBV associated with targeting (including changes in orientation, position, and velocity). This provision constrains the capability to simulate during flight tests the targeting and releasing of more reentry vehicles than permitted. The arms control effect is to restrain the ability to test a greater number of highly accurate reentry vehicles than currently carried (and currently accounted for in target survivability plans), and therefore limits the capability to deploy more reentry vehicles than would threaten missiles in hardened targets.

Another possible approach would be to establish through negotiation a normalized test-flight staging profile for missiles by agreeing to general parameters for thrust, boost, and (where appropriate) PBV burn times, normalized to parameters consistent with a second-strike retaliatory mission. By setting constraints on these parameters during flight testing it would be possible to control the type of delivery mission, e.g., second strike as opposed to hard target. Combined with flight test restraints on PBV maneuvers, a normalized staging profile could effectively restrain further development of destabilizing missions, depending, of course, on the parameters of the staging profile chosen as the standard.

Test Restrictions as a Means of Controlling R&D

Restrictions on weapon tests would represent a first step toward a comprehensive regime for establishing control over the pace of development of operational technology. These measures could (1) limit the pace of development and deployment of new systems, (2) lower the confidence of either side in its ability to carry out a successful surprise first strike, and (3) make verification easier by formulating monitoring tasks in terms of a "yes/no" decision as opposed to the more difficult "how much" decision.[2]

Another important advantage of these test restrictions is to draw a distinct line between R&D testing and field testing. New ideas can be researched in the lab (thereby maintaining a technological hedge), while full-scale tests of complete operational systems would be restricted with respect to which characteristics would be continued beyond R&D tests into the applied development phase preceding IOT&E and how fast they would be pursued.

Such a distinction between R&D testing and field testing is a necessary step in order to introduce arms control considerations into the weapons planning process. As it has been practiced to date, arms control concerns are most often taken into account only after a particular capability has substantially reached the applied development or field testing stage. The effect has often been twofold—first, the changes in specifications required by arms control have come at a phase in the weapons program in which it is expensive to redesign or retool major subsystems or components; and second, it is counterproductive for both arms control and weapons effectiveness since the "fix" is usually an unhappy compromise which is neither good arms control (not verifiable, does not constrain capability) nor good weapons design (erodes performance, reinforces bad engineering).

Permitting R&D testing is essential in order to avoid surprises from new technological breakthroughs and to add to basic knowledge. Basic knowledge about how new weapon technologies function is necessary in order to assess similar developments by other parties, and as part of the knowledge necessary for sound and durable arms control restraints if necessary. Particularly under the reality of increasingly complex and sophisticated systems, without such knowledge the chances of developing arms control proposals that effectively restrain destabilizing capabilities are lowered.

A real constraint on development programs would be to negotiate sharp reductions on the number and type of permitted flight tests (e.g., by 50 percent or more). Historically, both Soviet and U.S. missile test programs have been tending to rely on test flights programs consisting of fewer tests per year than previous years (see Table 6-1).

By further reducing the number of flight tests, one could also reduce the confidence of military commanders that the designated system would perform as designed or planned. In the case of hard-target, first-strike weapons, the reduction in the number of permitted flight tests would have two results:

1. Stretch out the time required to deploy a system that is considered operationally reliable in order to allow the other side to have greater confidence that it would have ample time to develop a similar system or appropriate countermeasures.
2. Retard confidence in the system's performance and reliability at the level needed for such missions, which is much higher than for retaliation against countervalue or soft military targets.

TABLE 6-1.
Summary of U.S. Missile Flight Tests, 1964–1979

Year	64	65	66	67	68	69	70	71	72	73	74	75	76	77	78	79	Total
Minuteman II																	
R&D	4	11	11	17	8	10			3	1	2	2					69
Basic Training			3		5	2											10
Operational tests						13	26	17	7	5	5	2	7	3	3		88
Total	4	11	14	17	13	25	26	17	10	6	7	4	7	3	3		167
Minuteman III																	
R&D					2	13	14	4	3	4	5	4	4	4	3	1	61
Basic Training							3	3									6
Operational tests								10	11	6	6	7	7	9	7	2	65
Total					2	13	17	17	14	10	11	11	11	13	10	3	132

U.S. SLBM Flight Tests

	Successes	Failures	Total
Polaris A1, A2, A3			
Flat pad launches (1961–1963)	34	8	42
DASO (1963–1967)			
A1	21	15	36
A2	38	5	43
A3	44	2	46
Operational tests	(Initially 20 per year, from 1974 about 5 per year.)		
Poseidon C-3			
Flat pad launches (1968–1970)	14	6	20
DASO (1971–1972)	23	5	28
Operational tests (1972–1980)	10	14	24
	(Tests continue at about 20 per year.)		
Trident C-4			
Flat pad launches (1977–1979)	14	4	18
RV flight series (1974–1977)	4	0	4
DASO (1979–1980)	6	1	7
Operational tests (1979–1980)	15	2	17

Source: Hussein Farooq, "The Impact of Weapons Test Restrictions," Adelphi Paper no. 165 (London: IISS, Spring 1981); see also M. Einhorn, G. Kane, and M. Nincic, "Strategic Arms Control Through Test Restraints," in *International Security* 8, no. 3 (1983):108.

The combined effect would be a return to confidence in second-strike weapons, a firmer basis for ensuring peaceful intent than hard-target, first-strike weapons.

We can illustrate simply how a limit on flight tests might stretch out the time before achieving a required confidence level in performance. Flight tests determine, among such other important quantities as reliability, the accuracy of a missile in hitting its target. Accuracy is frequently expressed in terms of the missile's circular error probable, or CEP, which is a statistical measure of ballistic missile accuracy. The CEP measures the distance from a chosen target within which, on average, one-half the total number of launched warheads will impact. Another very important quantity to planners is their *confidence* in achieving a certain accuracy or CEP. Confidence in achieving a measured value of the CEP for a given missile system improves with increasing numbers of tests, N, but the *rate* at which it improves increases relatively slowly with the square root of the number of tests; or, more accurately, as $1/(N-1)^{1/2}$. We can illustrate this effect by computing the estimated CEP in which we have 90 percent confidence — defined here as the upper-bound CEP — and comparing it to the actual measured CEP for different numbers of test shots. Their ratio is illustrated in Figure 6-1, for which the numerical values are computed on the basis of the following specific assumptions: (1) each coordinate of the miss distance is distributed normally, and (2) the mean and standard deviation remain constant throughout the test series. (The specific distribution for missile CEP estimates resulting from a finite number of tests depends on the characteristics of the missile tested. The one shown involves a single RV system with the miss distribution assumed to be circular [in order to give equal weight to both cross-range and down-range components]. The upper-bound CEP would be greater if the distribution of miss distances were elliptic with a larger down-range component. It may be lower for a given number of missile test firings for MIRVs since more RVs would be measured per firing. On the other hand, this statistical improvement may be countered by new systematic effects arising from dispensing of the MIRVs.)

Based on this curve showing how the 90 percent confidence upper-bound CEP decreases with the number of tests, it is possible to calculate how much delay an annual testing limit would have on achieving a given hard-target capability and the corresponding confidence degradation. For example, twelve tests per year represent current typical

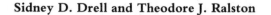

Figure 6-1
90% CONFIDENCE
ESTIMATED CEP/MEASURED CEP

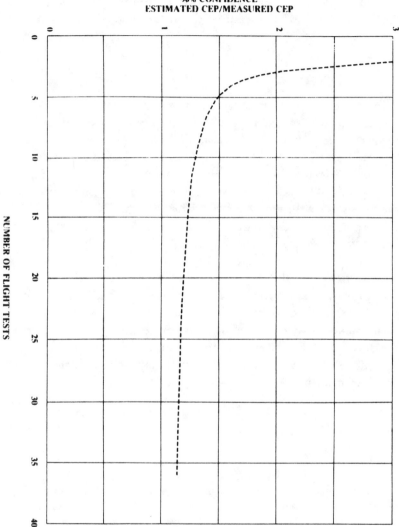

practice for a missile system in development. The figure shows that twelve tests bring the 90 percent confidence bound to within 30 percent of the measured CEP, that is, the upper bound is about 30 percent more than the measured CEP. A test limit of six flights per year would delay reaching such a goal in a new system by one year. A fixed annual ICBM test quota of six ICBM flights a year would clearly cause a very substantial delay. Furthermore, changes in equipment or manufacturing procedures over a several-year period could mean that the necessary high confidence in the measured CEP would not, in practice, ever be achieved.

CONCLUSION

A partial regime of test flight restrictions has already been negotiated successfully in SALT II. The provisions concerning the definition of new types of ICBMs restrict the *number* of flight tests allowed to the one new type of ICBM (twenty-five, the first twelve of which define the system, the final thirteen define the parameters of the system as those of the one new type). SALT II also took some tentative steps toward restrictions on the *type* of tests through constraints on PBV maneuvers in addition to constraints on growth greater than 10 percent variance in SALT parameters, i.e., launch weight, throw weight, length, and diameter, and a requirement for prior notification of tests.

In the final analysis, confidence is built by assuring each party that its forces are maintained and developed in a manner that guarantees it will be able to retaliate effectively, while at the same time permitting the maintenance of an R&D capability to avoid technological surprise. The measures described would contribute to the maintenance of this deterrent, and it is primarily in this role that they can be called confidence-building measures.

NOTES

1. In the United States this stage actually consists of three phases: (1) *basic research* in fields relevant to the technology (physics, chemistry, mathematics, electronics, etc.) — referred to in DOD budget parlance as "6.1 money" (package six, R&D Category 1, research); (2) exploratory development — application of basic science to potential applications (6.2); and (3) advanced development — implementation of the concepts worked out in 6.2.

2. A "yes/no" decision is a determination that a particular prohibited activity has or has not taken place. It is considered to be easier to detect the fact of the activity than it is to measure "how much" a particular prohibition on a performance parameter had been exceeded. Needless to say, there are cases when both can be difficult.

7 | The Military Significance of Restrictions on the Operations of Strategic Nuclear Forces

Alan J. Vick and James A. Thomson

A CONFIDENCE-BUILDING MEASURE (CBM) is any arms control measure that does not directly reduce, change, or limit the size or structure of forces. CBMs can range from agreements on the nonuse of force to those constraining the level of peacetime weapons testing or military maneuvers.

The CBMs discussed here deal with the operations of strategic nuclear forces. The broad goal of such measures would be to reduce the chance of nuclear warfare by helping to improve strategic deterrence and crisis stability.

Most discussion of CBMs has concentrated on clarifying the purposes of activities by conventional forces in central Europe. The Final Act of the 1975 Helsinki Conference on Security and Cooperation in Europe (CSCE) encourages signatory states to give a twenty-one day notification of ground force maneuvers in Europe of 25,000 or more troops and to invite observers from all signatory states. Most Western observers have been dissatisfied with this CBM, arguing that it lacks military significance; compliance is voluntary, rather than compulsory; and in any case, verification of compliance is difficult.

These concerns have led to several proposals for improved CBMs in the European theater. Most noteworthy are the Western "associated

The authors wish to thank their RAND colleagues Morlie Graubard, Kevin Lewis, and John Van Oudenaren for their helpful criticism and suggestions. This work was supported in part by the Ford Foundation.

measures" proposals in the Vienna negotiations on Mutual and Balanced Force Reductions (MBFR) and similar proposals in the Conference on Disarmament in Europe, which is confined to "Confidence and Security Building Measures" in its initial phases. In general, CBMs proposed by NATO countries in these contexts have sought to meet the NATO-developed criterion of "military significance" that was established because of dissatisfaction with the Helsinki Final Act. More specifically, the Western proposals seek the following:

1. Transparency—increase knowledge and understanding about force size, structure, and activities. Achievement of this goal would reduce uncertainties about either (a) current capabilities, thereby lessening possibilities for miscalculation based upon faulty analysis of the other side's capabilities, or (b) force operations in periods of tension, thereby reducing possibilities for misunderstandings and provocative counteractions.
2. Restraint—impede the ability to use force when intended for direct invasion or simply for intimidation.
3. Warning—enhance crisis decision-making, increasing the ability of both sides either to collect warning indicators or to determine whether specific actions implied warlike intentions. This goal, like the others, is usually pursued through agreements that would place barriers on the road to war. These would either lengthen the time needed to prepare for attack or would add political weight to judgments made about the importance of certain warning indicators.

In this chapter we explore the possibilities for extending such concepts for "militarily significant" theater CBMs into the realm of strategic intercontinental nuclear forces. Some precedents include the following:

1. The 1963 "Hot Line" Agreement
2. The 1971 Agreement on Measures to Reduce the Risk of Outbreak of Nuclear War Between the United States and Union of Soviet Socialist Republics
3. The SALT II requirement that the other signatory be notified prior to multiple ICBM launches
4. President Reagan's 1982 proposal for notification of *all* missile launches

Many proposals for strategic CBMs have been made in the open literature on arms control and strategic planning.[1] Our review of these proposals indicates that they cover many possible objectives, ranging from improved U.S.–Soviet relations to more specific military goals. Although CBMs may serve other objectives, we have limited this analysis to measures designed to be militarily significant—to have a real impact on the ability of each side to achieve military objectives. Careful attention to the military implications of these measures is thus essential to ensure that the U.S. ability to deter and, if necessary, to prosecute a war would not be adversely affected were they to be implemented.

Our analysis of the influence of strategic CBMs on American security interests assumes that antagonism between the Soviet Union and the United States will remain a basic international fact of life for any period such a regime would cover. This is an important factor influencing the evaluation of these proposals.

OBJECTIVES

In the realm of restrictions on the operations of strategic nuclear forces, we have defined two goals for militarily significant CBMs:

1. To reduce ambiguities in the operations of strategic force that might trigger military actions. This goal is similar to the "transparency" goal of theater CBMs.
2. To place barriers in the way of enhanced readiness for strategic force operations. Such barriers would potentially restrain nations from using force readiness as a tool of political intimidation or as a step toward preemptive nuclear attack. Because it is more readily analyzed, we have concentrated our efforts on reducing the possibilities for preemption, mindful that such measures also would reduce possibilities for political intimidation. Thus, this goal is similar to both the "restraint" and "warning" goals of theater CBMs.

The first goal would be addressed by restrictions and agreements that increased each side's knowledge and understanding of the predictability of its adversary's training and deployment procedures. Knowing just what constitutes "normal" operations goes a long way toward reducing suspicions generated by ambiguous operations. Although unilateral intelligence collection and analysis can provide much of this understanding, the exchange of observers, the notification of aircraft and ship movements, and the exchange of basic data on the operations of strategic forces could increase confidence in this body of knowledge. Such measures would do more than simply increase the information flow. They also would help both analysts and decision-makers make sense of otherwise perplexing activities.

Nevertheless, there could be problems. "If states focus on and become too familiar with the 'normal' pattern, they may become increasingly unable to discern warning indicators which are concealable in the pattern, and CBMs may even be exploited for concealment as more events become explicable in terms of the complexity of the normal pattern."[2]

Additionally, information needs differ substantially between the Soviet Union and the United States because of the closed nature of Soviet society and the openness of U.S. society. Furthermore, democracies in general may be more susceptible to the sort of deception previously mentioned. Consequently, it would be difficult to negotiate measures that have symmetrical effects. Such negative considerations, as well as their putative benefits, need to be considered in analyses of potential CBMs aimed at reducing ambiguities in strategic operations.

The second goal would be addressed by agreements that placed barriers on the road to war. In this concept, the agreements would not necessarily add to one's ability to collect warning indicators but would either (1) lengthen the time needed to prepare for an attack or (2) add political weight to judgments made about the significance of certain warning indicators. To explain the latter point: If an agreement must be breached on the road to attack (or more specifically to strategic nuclear attack), then the indicator associated with the agreement breach ought to carry more weight with decision-makers than if there were no agreement. For example, deployment of large numbers of SSBNs in a CBM-free world might be explained away for various reasons. If an agreement had been reached to limit the number of SSBNs deployed at any one time, however, political leaders would take the deployment of a number sufficient to violate the CBM more seriously. That, at least, is the theory. If designed with care, restrictions aimed at this goal could improve the survivability of strategic weapons and command facilities that are currently vulnerable because they depend on tactical warning for their survival. Of course, there are times when increased nervousness is warranted. If CBMs produced a false sense of security when alarm bells should have been ringing, they could encourage rather than deter surprise attack.

Improved tactical warning is an intermediate step to the more fundamental goal of deterrence. Because action upon tactical warning can improve survivability, it increases the U.S. (and Soviet) ability to employ strategic forces according to their missions, thereby contributing to deterrence.[3] The CBM regime must be designed such that reasonable and necessary precautionary actions (such as dispersing bombers) are not prohibited; otherwise, the CBM would defeat its own purpose.

The second goal, with its connection to improved tactical warning, underlines one of the chief difficulties with the concept of CBMs for strategic operations. It is most applicable to scenarios that threaten the initiation of strategic warfare "out of the blue." Although guarding against such scenarios is clearly important, few would argue that they should dominate the national security planning agenda. More likely scenarios would feature strategic nuclear warfare evolving from combat in a theater of military operations. In such circumstances it is hard to imagine that agreed CBMs on strategic force operations would carry much weight.

Proposals

In the context of the two broad goals outlined here, optional restrictions could limit deployments, training, or warhead handling or require notification of certain deployments, training, or types of operations. This analysis considers restrictions falling into three categories:

1. The size, location, and type of deployment (including launches of orbital vehicles) and notification of allowable deployments. Such restrictions would prohibit deployments that would reduce tactical warning and clarify otherwise ambiguous operations.
2. The size, location, and type of training missions (including command exercises) and notification of upcoming allowable training. These restrictions or notification would build confidence by lessening fears that such training would actually constitute an attack or mask attack preparations.

3. The handling and storage of warheads and their separation from launchers. These restrictions would increase tactical warning by adding a complex, observable step to the list of attack preparations.

In the next section we examine the peacetime force structure and operating procedures of the components of American and Soviet strategic nuclear forces—land-based intercontinental ballistic missiles (ICBMs), bombers, and strategic submarines (SSBNs). In addition, we discuss integrated force operations. The analysis asks whether there are ambiguities in component operations and what effect component operations have on tactical warning. In both cases we consider possible constraints on operations, addressing the following questions:

1. Can operational procedures be constrained without compromising force readiness?
2. If not, when do reductions in readiness threaten deterrence? (Initial small reductions in readiness may increase stability by making a surprise attack more difficult. However, radical reductions in readiness would decrease stability by undermining the survivability of the second-strike force.)

STRATEGIC FORCE OPERATIONS

Before identifying possible ambiguities in strategic force operations and evaluating the possible contributions of CBMs, it is necessary to consider the special characteristics of each of the legs of the strategic triad. In this section we survey operations of land- and sea-based missiles and long-range bombers.

Land-based Intercontinental Ballistic Missiles

U.S. and Soviet ICBMs are housed in hardened underground concrete and steel-reinforced silos and controlled by nearby underground launch control centers. In both the United States and the Soviet Union, ICBMs can be launched in a short period (on the order of a few minutes) with little visible preparation.[4]

Preparations for ICBM launches cannot be detected easily by the opponent, except for such blatant behavior as the movement of additional ICBMs next to silos, presumably to be reloaded into the silo after the initial strike. (This practice is prohibited by SALT II.) Perhaps the broadcast of launch orders would provide tactical warning. Unfortunately, no observable preattack stand-down is necessary. To ensure high reliability, however, the aggressor might conduct a massive and detailed evaluation and maintenance of his force before attacking. If so, there might be various warning indicators, ranging from unusual travel by senior officers of the Soviet Strategic Rocket Forces (SRF) or the U.S. Strategic Air Command (SAC) to exceptionally long hours of work by maintenance personnel.

Bombers

Both American and Soviet strategic bombers are deployed in wing-size elements at major operating bases in both countries. The United States also deploys one wing of B-52s at Andersen AFB, Guam. Both countries also have identified dispersal bases to increase the survival of bombers during wartime.

The American bomber force maintains a 30 percent alert rate. Aircraft on alert can be airborne six minutes after the pilots receive warning of attack.[5] Supporting elements of the strategic tanker force are on similar alert status. The Soviet alert level is not known, although it is probably lower in keeping with the Soviet propensity to maintain a low readiness profile in normal times.

Strategic Submarines

The American strategic submarine fleet operates out of Charleston, South Carolina, and Tacoma, Washington, with forward operating bases in Scotland and Guam.[6] These boats conduct deep-water patrols lasting sixty days, followed by thirty days in port. Transit time between port and patrol areas for the *Lafayette*-class submarines with "Poseidon" submarine–launched ballistic missiles (SLBMs) can range from one to six days, depending on the port. SSBNs equipped with the longer range "Trident I" SLBM generally enjoy shorter transit times to patrol areas.[7] During normal operations, approximately 50 percent of the force is on patrol at any one time.[8]

During normal operations, 80 to 90 percent of the Soviet strategic submarine fleet is in port at Severomorsk on the Kola Peninsula or at Petropavlovsk on the Kamchatka Peninsula.[9] When at sea, Soviet SSBNs patrol in the Barents Sea and the Sea of Okhotsk and off the American coasts.

Integrated Force Operations

Both the American and Soviet command-control-communications-intelligence (C³I) systems are composed of command posts, communication centers, data processing facilities, and intelligence collection/interpretation facilities. These systems are concerned primarily with monitoring friendly and enemy orders of battle and the more mundane, but equally vital, flow of personnel, equipment, and supplies that keep military facilities functioning. C³I operations support the National Command Authorities (NCA) by providing intelligence on enemy activities and communicating the directives of the NCA to the constituent forces. While the following discussion focuses on U.S. systems, one can assume that Soviet systems are similar.

The most observable elements of the strategic command and control system are the airborne command posts. In the United States they are the National Emergency Airborne Command Post (NEACP), the aircraft of the Post Attack Command and Communications System (PACCS), and the Take Charge and Move Out (TACAMO) aircraft of the U.S. Navy.

The NEACP fleet consists of four E-4A/B aircraft (converted Boeing 747s). One E-4 is always on ground alert, ready to meet members of the NCA at an appropriate location. The PACCS is composed of two squadrons of EC-135 aircraft dedicated to several missions. The first mission provides an airborne command post for the Commander-in-Chief of the Strategic Air Command. The remainder of the PACCS fleet are auxiliary command posts, radio-relay aircraft, or airborne launch control aircraft. TACAMO aircraft are converted C-130 transports that connect the NCA with the SSBN fleet by means of very low frequency communications. One TACAMO aircraft is on patrol over the Pacific and Atlantic at all times.

CBMs AND AMBIGUITIES IN FORCE OPERATIONS

In this section we identify several possible ambiguities in the operations of strategic forces that might be interpreted as hostile by the adversary. We then consider how restrictions on force operations might build confidence in the benign nature of these operations, evaluating both their possible positive contributions and their potential for abuse.

Ambiguities in ICBM Operations

The consistent high readiness of modern ICBM forces reduces the potential for misunderstandings about ICBM operations. ICBMs are unambiguously ready for war. The chief area for concern is that of testing, because detection of unannounced tests may be mistaken for an attack. Multiple missile tests and tests from operational silos by the Soviets have caused consternation in the United States. In particular, the 1982 Soviet multiple test of SS-11s, SS-20s, SLBMs, and ABMs could have been mistaken for an attack.[10] The United States does not test from operational silos.

One promising CBM would follow President Reagan's suggestion that all missile tests be announced beforehand. His proposal would decrease the ambiguity associated with unannounced tests. A 1983 *New York Times* article reported that Soviet members of the CBM working group in the START negotiations also proposed such notification.[11] Another possible CBM would prohibit all multiple launches. This is attractive because it would increase Soviet uncertainties associated with the coordination of a salvo attack, discouraging such attacks. Prohibition of multiple launches also would reduce the potential for accidental war, because integrated tests (e.g., the 1982 Soviet test) resemble an actual attack profile—the side detecting the multiple test might perceive it as an attack and respond by launching its own vulnerable ICBMs on warning. The prohibition of multiple tests would reduce this possibility.

Ambiguities in Bomber Operations

Both the United States and the Soviet Union have identified dispersal bases to increase aircraft survival during war, and the Soviets have built Arctic staging areas to make maximum use of the limited striking radius of medium-range bombers. Both nations conduct Arctic training flights. Although use of Arctic bases is not necessarily provocative, such actions in conjunction with a massive stand-down of the bomber force and large-scale dispersal might cause concern.

Flight Notification

One CBM for bomber operations thus would require that all movements of aircraft above some threshold number be announced in advance, along with major bomber training exercises. The Soviets are reported to have proposed notification of all mass bomber takeoffs.[12] No dramatic military costs would result from such measures, which would reduce the potential for misunderstanding without hindering training or readiness. As with any CBM, however, a potential would exist for creating a false sense of confidence. The Soviets might announce a major exercise as a cover for a real attack by bombers. Although a first strike led by hundreds of bombers is not considered plausible, smaller attacks might successfully use a major exercise for cover.

Another proposal attributed to the Soviets would prohibit bomber operations near the adversary's borders. Detection of adversary bombers near one's borders is cause for alarm and might result in provocative countermeasures. A measure prohibiting these operations might lessen the potential for misunderstandings.

More generally, however, to the extent that periodic bomber training operations help maintain the U.S. capability to penetrate Soviet air defenses, they contribute to the viability of the bomber component of the Triad. The CBMs described previously should be evaluated in terms of their effect on U.S. deterrent capabilities because there may be a tradeoff between reducing the chances for misunderstanding through CBMs and maintaining the deterrent value of bombers.

Stand-downs

A large-scale bomber attack might be preceded by an extensive force stand-down for maintenance. Consequently, detection of such actions may be considered strategic warning of attack. To preclude misunderstandings, each nation could agree to notify the other of all aircraft stand-downs affecting more than a certain percentage of the force. Detection of an unnotified stand-down, of course, would then have greater weight as a warning indicator. This appears to be a reasonable and useful CBM.

Ambiguities in SSBN Operations

Deployments of strategic submarines near the adversary's coasts can produce misunderstandings over possible uses of these strategic platforms. For example, the submarines might attack the nation's command and control system or bombers based in coastal areas before precautionary measures could be taken to reduce the vulnerability of these assets. The short flight time of ballistic missiles launched from these submarines makes such attacks at least theoretically possible. Since both nations have reason to fear such deployments, they would increase the incentives for preemption. Any forward deployment of SSBNs is ambiguous to some degree.

Notification of deployments might help reduce concern about such operations, although they also might produce false confidence. A few SSBNS can do great damage, so notification becomes less appealing because any deployment is threatening. It might increase confidence that a massive attack was not planned but would offer little insurance against small attacks.

Ambiguities in Integrated Force Operations

Any combined force operation supported by unusual NCA activities might produce anxiety in the other nation. In particular, staffing at higher than routine levels of airborne or land-based command posts, unusual radio traffic, or unexplained absences of key members of the National Command Authorities (NCA) all might be misconstrued as warning of attack.

Any of these events are cause for concern, particularly if associated with changes in force deployments. However, they do not appear individually to be amenable to CBMs. And, given concern for communications security, it seems unlikely that either side would be willing to notify the other of command post exercises.

Large-scale field exercises cannot be hidden, however, and communications associated with these observable events are likely to receive considerable scrutiny even without notification. A requirement to notify the other side of integrated force exercises that included a field component may therefore be a fruitful area for CBMs. Such notification might reduce concerns about these activities, and the military cost appears small. Indeed, President Reagan proposed such a requirement in 1982. Additionally, a channel for the clarification of ambiguous C³ activities, perhaps below the presidential level, might be useful in reducing the chances for misunderstanding.

Prospects for Reducing Ambiguities

Ambiguities in force operations appear most amenable to confidence-building because they generally can be clarified through simple notification measures. Indeed, some measures (e.g., test notifications and bomber stand-downs) are so straightforward that one might ask why they are not observed unilaterally. Of course, neither country may be particularly concerned about such operations, each trusting its national intelligence services to distinguish between threatening and routine operations, and these seemingly innocuous measures may be of little military significance.

CBMs and Tactical Warning

In this section we discuss the dependence of some strategic force components on warning for their survival, the threats posed by specified weapon systems, and potential measures to increase the survival of these warning-dependent systems. For each such weapon system we ask: Does this weapon pose a special threat (one not posed by any other element of the triad) to some component of the opponent's strategic forces? If not, does it pose *any* threat to warning-dependent systems? This section emphasizes submarine operations because the submarine component of U.S. and Soviet strategic forces was the only one that posed a special threat that appeared amenable to a host of CBMs. We devote most of our effort to discussing these potential measures.

Force Vulnerabilities

As we discussed earlier, our second goal for CBMs is to place barriers in the way of enforced readiness for attack. Thus by increasing the probability and length of tactical warning of attack, CBMs may be able to reduce the vulnerability of bombers and, perhaps, the NCA to surprise attack. The vulnerability of ICBMs and SSBNs seems less amenable to improvements via CBMs.

Both U.S. and Soviet silo-based ICBMs can be destroyed only by a coordinated, massive attack using high-yield, very accurate weapons. While the Soviet Union already possesses sufficient numbers of such weapons to destroy a large portion of our ICBMs, in a pre-emptive attack, the United States is not projected to have a comparable capability until the early 1990s. Nevertheless, both countries are already seeking solutions to this vulnerability. For example, ICBMs may be deployed on mobile vehicles. Such vehicles would depend mainly on the other side's uncertainty about their location for survival. Tactical warning might be used to increase this area of uncertainty and particularly to raise it beyond the abilities of the attacker to saturate the area with lethal amounts of weapons. If this tactic were chosen, the survivability of land-based ICBMs would be tied to timely tactical warning.

SSBNs at sea are currently invulnerable to attack by strategic nuclear forces, and submarines in port are not maintained on high alert.[13] Neither the survival of the patrolling submarines nor the destruction of submarines in port is a function of tactical warning (although submarines in port could be rushed to sea upon strategic warning).

Both the United States and the Soviet Union maintain a portion of their strategic bomber forces on alert. These aircraft depend on tactical warning for survival. The remainder of the force depends on strategic warning to disperse and increase alert rates. Optimally located submarines deployed near the opponent's coasts executing an intricate, highly coordinated barrage attack on bomber bases[14] may be able to destroy the alert bombers also. This potential is a function of the shortened flight time of a ballistic missile launched from a submarine in coastal waters. In some cases, particularly for American bomber bases, this flight time may be as low as six minutes. Alert bomber crews need approximately this much time to take off. All bombers may therefore be vulnerable in such a first strike.

Both the United States and the Soviet Union deploy airborne command posts for control of their strategic nuclear forces. In the United States, one such aircraft is airborne at all times so the command and control of at least one retaliatory strike may not be dependent on tactical warning. Other elements of the PACCS are on ground alert and would be threatened by any attack equivalent to the attack on bomber forces previously discussed.[15] The NEACP (upon tactical warning of ICBM attack) might be able to escape with the President and a few advisers on board. They could not escape an attack by forward-deployed SSBNs; however, survival of the President and other senior officials is predicated upon the timely receipt of strategic warning.

ICBMs and Tactical Warning

The high level of readiness of ICBM forces does not pose a special threat to most components of strategic forces during noncrisis operations. These components are either always vulnerable (fixed C³I assets and U.S. ICBMs), would require lengthy tactical or strategic warning to escape (nonalert bombers, in-port SSBNs, and the NCA), or are not vulnerable at all (alert bombers and patrolling SSBNs). The ICBM forces pose a special threat to such hard targets as opposing ICBM silos, but do not threaten warning-dependent systems any differently than do other elements of the triad. Yet they do pose a threat. We might therefore ask if any CBMs can reduce vulnerabilities to ICBM attacks, knowing that we would also have to address vulnerability to SSBN attack.

ICBM warheads could be stored separately from launchers, which would certainly make a first strike with ICBMs difficult. Perhaps even a few hours would be required to prepare for attack. Warhead separation would fulfill one goal of operational CBMs—to reduce readiness and increase tactical and strategic warning of attack.

On-site inspection would probably be required to ensure that warheads had not been remounted surreptitiously. Reliance solely on National Technical Means (NTM) of verification and other intelligence sources would entail high risks. If one side were planning an attack and the opponent detected each step in the preparations and responded in kind, the day of attack would find the attacker at 100 percent readiness and the "victim" at 100 percent readiness. An attack under these conditions would not be prudent. However, some of the attacker's preparations would probably go undetected or not be recognized as such. Even if hourly updates on the attacker's readiness were available, it is not clear that they would be viewed as unambiguous evidence of aggressive intent. Political pressures to avoid provocative counterbehavior, including increasing alert rates, might limit the "victim's" responses.

The separation of warheads from launch vehicles would make ICBMs indirectly vulnerable to a first strike by SLBMs or bombers (assuming that mounting warheads was extremely time-consuming). If SLBM or bomber strikes destroyed warhead warehouses, the launchers would be useless. Also, the roads to the silos might be made impassable by cratering or destroying transport vehicles. Indeed, ICBMs might become more vulnerable through such restrictions.

In sum, warhead separation for ICBMs alone looks like a bad idea. Yet if SLBM, ICBM, and bomber warheads were separated under a verifiable agreement, concern over first strikes could be dramatically lessened.

Bomber Operations and Tactical Warning

Current bomber operations pose no threat to systems dependent upon warning for survival. Deployment of "stealth" bombers may change this, however. It may be instructive therefore to consider CBMs to increase warning of bomber attack.

The separation of warheads from bombers is an option that would make a first strike more difficult, adding a potentially observable step in war preparations. Yet, as a percentage of bomber flight time, warhead separation would make only a trivial addition to tactical warning. In any case, few analysts are concerned about a bomber first strike.

Such restrictions also would hinder the use of strategic bombers in the pursuit of broad American foreign policy interests. In a few cases since 1948, the United States has relied on "nuclear" bombers to make implicit threats and to support conventional operations (an airborne equivalent to Navy carrier task force "show the flag" missions). If the Soviets or their allies knew that American nuclear warheads were separated from the bombers, per a formal treaty, one of two negative results would obtain. A demonstration fly-by of a B-52 known to be unarmed (or at least lacking nuclear weapons) would be an empty gesture. Alternatively, arming B-52 aircraft with nuclear weapons in violation of a treaty would be a highly provocative move, guaranteed to generate much criticism at home and abroad.

We conclude that bomber warhead separation would at best be of little value as a tool to increase tactical warning and in the extreme might conflict with broader security interests of the United States.

Another option would require basing bombers in the southern part of each country. This CBM would stem from the desire to maximize the distance that bombers have to fly on strategic missions. Since long-range bombers are expected to fly polar routes, it is advantageous militarily to base them along the northern borders. This is particularly important for the Soviet Union since the distance between its northern and southern parts is considerable and because one of its most modern and capable bombers, the Backfire, has somewhat limited range. Northern staging airfields thus can play a critical role in preparations for attacks or even as refueling stops if air-to-air refueling assets were limited.

Specifically, this CBM would prohibit the peacetime basing of medium- and long-range bombers at forward bases. Current facilities in the northern zones could be maintained and limited flights might even be allowed, but no basing or maintenance of aircraft would be allowed. This restriction could increase tactical warning by making the forward deployment of bombers to northern staging areas an additional observable step in the preparation for war. Although this CBM would have the collateral effect of increasing bomber flight time in route to targets, few would view this increase as strategically significant. In any event, this effect would be secondary to the more important improvement in warning.

This is a fairly innocent measure and appears worth consideration. Nevertheless, some problems should be noted. Bomber bases are not inexpensive. To the extent that northern facilities are fully developed major operating bases, there may be reluctance to spend the hundreds of millions of dollars necessary to build new bases. The likely result in the United States would be further crowding of existing bases in southern states. Since many of these bases are in coastal areas, such a redeployment might increase bomber vulnerability to attacks by ballistic missiles launched from submarines. As a general point, dispersal is always preferred over concentration; it complicates attack planning, increases overall survivability, and provides safer, faster fly-outs. Thus, the appeal of this measure is related to its impact on bomber dispersal within the areas allowed.

SSBN Operations and Tactical Warning

Soviet SSBNs forward deployed to within 2,000 kilometers of the American coast would be able to attack several SAC bases simultaneously, destroying the alert force on the ground or within seconds of takeoff (by means of an area barrage of nuclear weapons exploded in the air). Why is this the case? During normal peacetime operations the SAC B-52 alert forces, 30 percent of the bomber fleet, require six minutes of warning for the crews to run from their shelters, board the aircraft, and take off.[16] Optimally located, forward-deployed SSBNs can put weapons onto targets in less than six minutes. A Soviet SLBM launched 2,000 kilometers away from an airfield would detonate just as the alert force took off. Airbursts in the vicinity would disable or destroy some of the aircraft that managed to escape.

An SLBM need not actually arrive this quickly because the six-minute figure did not include the time necessary to detect an attack and communicate that fact to the authorities able to order the aircraft to take off. In fact, early warning satellites in geostationary orbits must detect the launch and relay this information through ground stations to the SAC alert system; a decision would then have to be made by CINCSAC or the NCA to flush the bombers.[17] Such a decision would not carry the weight of, say, a presidential decision to launch the ICBM force on warning of attack, because the bombers would return to base if they did not subsequently receive an authorized attack order. Although a decision to flush bombers would be precautionary and would not imply a decision to initiate nuclear war, it still would take some time for the decision process to be completed. One would not launch bombers casually. It might even take several minutes for this entire detection-communication-decision-communication sequence to be completed. If so, any SSBN within ten minutes flight time would threaten air bases. Indeed, two SSBNs (each equipped with sixteen SS-N-18 missiles, for example), 1,000 kilometers off each coast, would together be able to attack every air base in the United States with less than ten minutes warning.[18] In other words, two Soviet *Delta*-class submarines equipped with SS-N-18s[19] could attack an entire component of the U.S. triad.

Additionally, forward-deployed SSBNs could threaten the American NCA with surprise destruction because there would be no way to evacuate key members upon warning of an attack. Even if helicopters were kept on ground alert at Andrews AFB, it would require sixteen minutes to make a round trip to the White House (and this figure does not include loading time or the takeoff run for the NEACP).[20] During a crisis, helicopters could be kept on alert at the Pentagon, White House, etc., reducing flight time to eight minutes. With loading and warning sequences factored in, evacuation could occur some ten to twenty minutes after the launch—still fatally late.

American SSBNs forward-deployed in the Mediterranean, Laptev, Barents, and Kara seas and in the Sea of Japan could launch a similar attack on the Soviet Union. Although Soviet geography would force the United States to use more SSBNs,[21] their NCA and bomber forces appear as vulnerable as ours.

Cruise Restrictions

One approach in addressing these vulnerabilities would restrict the number of SSBNs allowed to leave port and would require notification of such cruises. The advantage would be twofold: restricting the number of boats at sea would limit the number of targetable reentry vehicles (RVs); the reduced number, combined with notification of cruises, would make the opposition's antisubmarine task easier, lessening concerns about unaccounted-for SSBNs. A first strike by forward-deployed SSBNs against the NCA and bombers alone is unlikely. It is more probable that other targets—launch control facilities, ICBM silos, military installations, the entire gamut of C^3 assets, nuclear weapon facilities, railroad yards, and ports—would come under ICBM and SLBM attack. If so, it would be necessary to deploy a fair number of boats at sea and flush the remainder out of the highly vulnerable docking facilities, which would undoubtedly come under ICBM and SLBM attack within minutes of the first strike.

Without a CBM restricting deployments, the dispersion of an SSBN force to sea could always be explained as an exercise. The existence of a CBM prohibiting such activities, on the other hand, would add tremendous political weight to any warning that a deployment were indeed occurring.

Although these advantages do recommend CBMs limiting deployments of SSBNs, several problems would arise. The first relates to SSBN survival. Reducing the number of SSBNs at sea would place both cruising and in-port submarines at greater risk. The fewer SSBNs at sea, the easier they would be to track. Consequently, they might become more vulnerable to attack by ASW forces. The advantage to one side would be a liability to the other. SSBNs in port of course would be vulnerable to SLBM or ICBM attacks.

The second problem relates to the effectiveness of limitations on SSBN deployments in preventing, discouraging, or, at the least, mitigating the consequences of a strike against time-urgent targets such as the NCA and alert bombers. Although each nation has confidence in its ability to detect rapid, large deployments of enemy SSBNs, there is no similar confidence in abilities to guarantee that no single SSBN escaped the ASW net. Leakage, so troublesome in all defenses against nuclear forces, cannot be escaped.

If one SSBN were deployed surreptitiously and remained undetected, it could take out the opposition's command authorities and many bomber bases. The Soviets, for example, might count on the confusion surrounding the destruction of U.S. national command authorities to delay any American retaliation for the thirty minutes it would take for Soviet ICBMs, launched after the SSBN attack, to arrive and destroy U.S. land-based missiles and the remainder of fixed C³ assets. In such a case, the United States would have little residual nuclear capability left. Although such a scenario presents nightmarish uncertainties and dangers for the Soviet Union, it does illustrate the sensitivity of CBMs to verification capabilities.

An American submarine in the Norwegian, Baltic, or Mediterranean Sea also could decapitate the Soviet NCA in Moscow and destroy in-port submarines on the Kola Peninsula and many bomber bases. Another American SSBN in the Sea of Japan could take out many more bomber bases, air defense sites, and Soviet SSBNs at Petropavlovsk. Although their greater number of warheads would allow U.S. submarines to attack more targets than Soviet SSBNs, the American SSBNs could not reach interior bomber bases. The current American lack of silo-busting ICBMs, furthermore, would allow more Soviet ICBMs to survive a full first strike than American ICBMs under a Soviet attack on the United States.

American planners thus are likely to object to restrictions on SSBN deployments for the very same reason they express concern about bomber survivability and the risk of surprise attacks on the national command authorities. They wish to ensure that American forces and command structures can survive any surprise attack. SSBN deployment restrictions might gain increased NCA and bomber survivability (viewed narrowly, from one attack scenario), but they would do so at the cost of increasing SSBN vulnerability to a surprise attack, whether by ASW forces at sea or by missile attacks on submarines in port. One kind of vulnerability would be added with no guarantee that the motivating vulnerability had been removed. Additionally, a certain amount of flexibility, military freedom, and operational secrecy would be given up.

Soviet planners should more readily agree to SSBN restrictions, viewing it as an opportunity to constrain American operational freedom while giving little in return. After all, the Soviets currently restrict 80 to 90 percent of their SSBN force to port. Soviet planners place great confidence in their ability to recognize the political and military events portending war. They would use a period of increasing tensions to prepare their forces for war. Under current conditions, American forward-deployed SSBNs do not cause great concern. If war appeared imminent, the Soviets would respond to such deployments with appropriate countermeasures (e.g., evacuation of the NCA, dispersal of strategic bombers, and, ultimately, preemptive attack) in an environment in which all CBMs would probably be irrelevant.

Keep-in Zones

An alternative way to hamper forward deployment of SSBNs would be to require that a body or a few bodies of water be designated as SSBN sanctuaries[22] and keep-in zones. SSBNs would be required to be either in-port, in-transit to a keep-in zone, or in the keep-in zones. In some cases, the port might be adjacent to a keep-in zone, requiring no transit time (and simplifying verification).

Each country would possess its own zone or zones, preferably in waters protected by its air and sea power. Opposing ASW forces would, in any case, be prohibited from operating in this zone. The zone would be protected by passive and active ASW arrays on the ocean floor, friendly attack submarines, ASW ships, helicopters, and fixed-wing aircraft. The SSBNs would patrol freely and randomly within this zone.

In addition to this ring of friendly antisubmarine forces, the opposing nation might want to operate an outer ASW ring to ensure that the SSBNs stay in the keep-in zone and not deploy forward. Thus, the SSBNs would be protected from opposition ASW and the opposition NCA and bombers would be protected from the SSBNs.

TABLE 7-1

Possible Soviet Sanctuaries

	Parts of the United States Reachable from the Sanctuary by		
Sanctuary	SS-N-6[a]	SS-N-8[b]	SS-N-18[c]
Sea of Okhotsk	Alaska	All	Most
East Siberian Sea	Alaska	All	All
Laptev Sea	Alaska (most)	All	All
Kara Sea	None	All	All
Barents Sea	None	All	All
Black Sea	None	Northeast U.S. (including D.C.)	Northeast U.S. (including D.C.)
Caspian Sea	None	Upper Northeast	New England
Number of SLBMs	400	292	208

Source: Ranges from IISS, *The Military Balance,* 1982-1983, London, 1983.
  [a]2,400-3,000-kilometer range
  [b]7,800-9,100-kilometer range
  [c]6,500-8,300-kilometer range

Possible keep-in zones for the Soviets include the Okhotsk, Siberian, Laptev, Kara, Barents, Black, and Caspian Seas. As Table 7-1 illustrates, the Black and Caspian can be ruled out because of range limitations. Any of the Arctic seas or the Sea of Okhotsk would be suitable for submarines carrying SS-N-8, SS-N-18, and SS-NX-20 SLBMs. The remainder of the Soviet fleet could be considered a reserve for deployment during war or as submarine-based theater weapons for use in the event of war against China or in Europe.

Okhotsk would be particularly attractive as a zone because of its natural choke points. It is virtually surrounded by the Soviet landmass, the Kamchatka Peninsula, Sakhalin Island, and the Kuril Islands. The limited number of passages could be easily monitored and defended, making penetration by enemy attack submarines difficult. Furthermore, the Soviets already possess a submarine base nearby at Petropavlovsk (on the Pacific), air bases on Sakhalin Island, and ground forces in the Kuril Islands. The Barents/White Sea also would be attractive as a combined sanctuary. There are massive ground, naval, and air forces on the Kola Peninsula and a submarine base at Severomorsk. Nearby facilities, local naval superiority, choke points (less so in the Barents), and size all would recommend these two zones. While at first blush it may appear that winter ice would reduce the attractiveness of these zones, recent reports of Soviet submarine deployments in the Arctic suggest that they view ice covered waters as ideal SSBN sanctuaries, conceivably protecting their submarines from surveillance.[23] This study will use these two zones as reference points. The actual choice of

TABLE 7-2

Possible U.S. Sanctuaries

Sanctuary	Parts of the Soviet Union Reachable from the Sanctuary by	
	Poseidon C-3[a]	Trident C-4[b]
Beaufort Sea	Northern S.U.	All
Baffin Bay	European Russia[c]	All
Hudson Bay	None	Most
Labrador Sea	European Russia[c]	Most
Gulf of St. Lawrence	None	Northern S.U.[c]
Great Lakes	None	Northern S.U.
Gulf of Mexico	None	Northeast Siberia
Gulf of California	None	Northeast Siberia
Number of SLBMS	304	216

Source: Ranges from IISS, *The Military Balance,* 1982-1983, London, 1983
[a]4,600-kilometer range
[b]7,400-kilometer range
[c]Including Moscow

zones would require a major study, incorporating considerations of ocean topography, the effects of nuclear explosions in the particular zones (particularly underwater explosions), the difficulty of enclosing an ASW screen, and other issues.

Possible keep-in zones for the United States would include the Beaufort and Labrador Seas, Baffin and Hudson Bays, Gulfs of Mexico and California, and the Great Lakes (see Table 7-2). Range limitations rule out all but the Beaufort Sea and Baffin Bay. Baffin is superior to Beaufort because of better choke points and because the C-3 SLBM can strike more important targets in European Russia from this zone than the Arctic wastelands it would reach from Beaufort. The C-4 SLBM can strike all targets in the Soviet Union from both zones.

To determine the utility of such control zones, we need to address the following questions:

1. Could the zone provide an increase in SSBN survivability greater than other options?
2. Could the zone reduce the probability of leakage that plagued the first proposal to restrict the number of forward deployments?

To answer the first question we consider three threats to SSBN survival.

1. Covert Insertion of Sensors into the Sanctuary. This problem is particularly acute for sanctuaries bordering potentially hostile territory or neutral territory that might be penetrated by special teams.[24] Examples of problem areas for the Soviet Union include the Okhotsk Sea (shared by the Japanese) and the Barents Sea (shared by Norway). American SSBNs using Baffin Bay would be surrounded by friendly Greenland and Canada, but the lack of inhabitants or major armed forces suggest that landing teams could probably penetrate. Insertion of sensors might occur by boat, aircraft, or submarine, or from shore. Obviously, special security arrangements would be required.

2. Eavesdropping by ASW Assets Outside of the Zone. This problem stems from the need for two ASW lines. The outer array might go beyond ensuring that SSBNs do not escape, actually tracking the movements of some SSBNs in the zone. One report suggests that current American sound surveillance (SOSUS) arrays near Norway's Bear Island can cover much of the Barents Sea.[25] Another report contains a map showing SOSUS arrays off the east coast of the United States and west

coast of Spain, providing coverage for the entire North Atlantic,[26] suggesting that the range of a single line may be as high as 3,000 kilometers. If true, then no zone can provide reliable protection for SSBNs. A zone capable of frustrating long-range detection would be ridiculously large, presenting an unmanageable ASW task for friendly forces. It is reasonable to expect each side to expend efforts to increase this eavesdropping potential, given the attractive intelligence that might be gained.

3. Focused ASW/New Technology. A zone would allow the opposition to focus ASW resources (which previously collected data from and observed tens of millions of square miles of ocean) on a fairly small body of water. That is not to say that worldwide tactical ASW efforts would cease, but the considerable assets devoted to tracking SSBNs could enjoy the products of concentrated efforts. The potent combination of recent advances in sensor technology and very high-speed data processing with a detailed data set from a more discrete area could very well yield new understanding of how submarines disturb their environments. Relationships that were not apparent through theory or experience on the open seas might be discovered in this way. Advances in sensor technology may permit detection of submarine wakes, chemical discharges, or acoustic disturbances at long ranges. Blue–green lasers might make the ocean transparent to satellite observation, allowing real-time tracking. At the least, concentrated observation and analysis is likely to lead to some reduction in location uncertainty, perhaps to the point that SSBNs could be destroyed.

Any of these possibilities might yield sufficient data to justify a barrage attack on the area of suspected activity. Although the zone was selected because its size would make a barrage attack costly, reductions in location uncertainty might make such an attack feasible.

Destruction of SSBNs by ICBM or SLBM warheads is not a trivial task. Warheads have to be designed specifically for water penetration and must detonate at a great enough depth to prevent the fireball from breaching the surface. A warhead reentering at the low velocity required to penetrate water would be, in effect, an aerodynamic vehicle and susceptible to winds, rain, and hail. It could not therefore possess great accuracy. Because many such warheads would be required for a barrage attack and would have limited value in other applications, the ICBM or SLBM force would suffer a considerable reduction in flexibility. Nevertheless, the dedication of many launchers to this task might be cost-effective in certain circumstances. Certainly, the use of such zones would channel research in this direction.

Finally, we need to determine whether such zones could reduce the potential for surreptitiously forward-deploying SSBNs. Current ASW abilities can guarantee that no massive escape of the SSBN force would be likely. Such zones could therefore provide great confidence that the opponent could not deploy many boats unobserved. Unfortunately, such confidence could not be held at low leakage levels. No current ASW system could guarantee that a few boats would not escape unobserved. Because bomber and NCA survivability would be highly sensitive to the leakage of even one boat, the prospects for such zones are not encouraging.

Keep-out Zones

A final proposal to consider is the keep-out zone, which would prohibit operations in certain provocative areas but otherwise would allow deployment at any level. SSBNs may patrol in any of the world's oceans. For our purposes, the keep-out zone would prohibit SSBNs off both nations' coasts. The sole purpose of such a zone would be to hinder surprise attacks against time-urgent targets. It in no way would restrict ASW operations and would not pretend to increase SSBN survivability.

The United States is certainly capable of building an elaborate detection system off its coasts to police such a zone. It reportedly already can track submarines throughout the North Atlantic.[27] Enforcement of a keep-out zone, however, would require more thorough coverage—the use of many attack submarines, ASW ships, helicopters, and long-range fixed-wing aircraft such as the P-3C Orion. Most of our current ASW assets would have to be devoted to the patrol of this zone. Many false targets (e.g., whales) would have to be investigated.

We could be no more confident that a few SSBNs would not slip into the keep-out zone than we were in the keep-in zone. Furthermore, an important geopolitical asymmetry exists. The Soviet Union could agree to a keep-out zone without seriously undermining its relationship with key allies. In contrast, a U.S. agreement to respect a 2,000 to 3,000-kilometer zone around the Soviet Union would necessitate removal from European waters of SSBNs dedicated to NATO. The NATO allies would not view such a move with favor. It could reduce the credibility of the American nuclear guarantee for Europe.

CONCLUSION

Confidence-building measures may be useful tools for reducing ambiguities about operations of strategic forces. They would be most productive as an information-sharing device. As discussed in this chapter, exchange of data on force operations, exchanges of observers, and requirement of prior notification of certain types of activities may contribute to strategic stability and deterrence without the high military costs associated with actual operational restrictions.

However, we are less hopeful about the role of confidence-building measures in increasing the probability, amount, and political impact of tactical warning of nuclear attack. Prohibiting bomber basing at northern staging airfields might provide a fairly unambiguous observable indication of bomber attack preparations. The problem of bomber and NCA vulnerability to SLBM attack does not, however, appear to be soluble by CBMs restricting SSBN operations; nevertheless, technical studies may offer solutions to some of the objections presented in our analysis.

Confidence-building measures thus simply are not powerful enough tools to shoulder a burden as great as ensuring the survival of nuclear forces. If the United States must deploy weapon systems that depend in some way on tactical warning for survival, then other means will be necessary to improve the timeliness and accuracy of such warning. Confidence-building measures may be useful for other purposes, but not this.

There may be a fundamental inconsistency between current Western deterrence doctrine and the notion of strategic confidence-building measures discussed here. The NATO extended deterrence concept—the link between the American strategic umbrella and Europe, as codified in the NATO strategy of flexible response—is predicated on maintaining uncertainty in the minds of Soviet leaders about the possibility that a NATO conventional war could escalate to strategic nuclear war. To the extent that the United States takes steps—unilaterally or bilaterally with the USSR—designed to reassure the Soviets that a crisis or conflict need not escalate, it may undermine its own deterrence concept. But in essence this is what strategic confidence-building measures would seek to do.

Thus, strategic force operations probably are not the most fertile field for confidence-building compared, for example, with theater force operations. If a chief goal of strategic CBMs is to reduce the risk of strategic nuclear war, then the likely context for the initiation of such a war should be considered. Few would argue that a strategic nuclear war would erupt out of the blue. It would more probably be initiated as a consequence of conventional (and then nuclear) conflict in a theater of military operations growing out of a grave political crisis. CBMs aimed more generally at reducing the risk of war have a better chance of building confidence than those aimed specifically at strategic nuclear war. Theater CBMs are therefore probably a more fertile field than strategic CBMs.

NOTES

1. See, for example, Alton Frye, "Building Confidence between Adversaries: An American's Perspective," in Karl Birnbaum (ed.), *Confidence Building and East-West Relations* (Laxenburg, Austria: Austrian Institute for International Affairs, 1983).

2. Johan J. Holst, "Confidence Building Measures: A Conceptual Framework," *Survival* (January/February 1983), p. 2.

3. A related goal is to provide sufficient indication of attack preparation or of a conditional decision by the opponent to strike in enough time to take steps designed to dissuade the aggressor from attacking. For example, if the defending nation responds promptly and vigorously with precautionary actions such as flushing bombers and SSBNs and alerting all other forces, the potential attacker might reverse the decision to attack. Such a reversal might be argued for because the defender's actions had reduced the chances for a successful strike.

4. Desmond Ball, "Can Nuclear War Be Controlled?" *Adelphi Paper #169* (London: International Institute for Strategic Studies, 1981), p. 42.

5. Norman Polmar, *Strategic Air Command: People, Aircraft, and Missiles* (Annapolis, Maryland: Nautical and Aviation Publishing Company of America, 1979), p. 55.

6. International Institute for Strategic Studies, *The Military Balance, 1982–1983* (London, 1983), p. 4.

7. Herbert Scoville, Jr., "Missile Submarines and National Security," *Scientific American* (June 1972).

8. See Joel Wit, "Advances in Anti-submarine Warfare," *Scientific American* (February 1981); and Patrick Sloyan, "Submarines May Lose Cloak of Darkness," *Los Angeles Times* (May 28, 1982).

9. Ray Bonds (ed.), *Russian Military Power* (New York: St. Martin's Press, 1980).

10. "Soviets' Integrated Test of Weapons," *Aviation Week and Space Technology* (June 28, 1982), pp. 20–21.

11. "U.S. and Soviet Seek to Prevent a Surprise Attack," *New York Times* (December 8, 1983), p.A.6.

12. Ibid.

13. If we stretch our definition of strategic force operations to include Antisubmarine Warfare (ASW) directed at SSBNs, then restrictions on ASW operations might be appropriately included. We decided that because considerable work has already addressed the issue of ASW restraints, we will not discuss such restraints except where they complement measures restricting strategic force operations per se. For more on ASW restrictions, see Richard Garwin, "Antisubmarine Warfare and National Security," *Scientific American* (July 1972).

14. In the United States, this number is quite small. There are twenty-three primary bomber bases and seventy dispersal bases. A small number of forward-deployed SSBNs could launch sufficient warheads to destroy these targets. See Alton Quanbeck and Archie L. Wood, *Modernizing the Strategic Bomber Force: Why and How,* (Washington, D.C.: The Brookings Institution, 1976), p. 24.

15. Ball, 1981, p. 16.

16. Polmar, 1979, p. 55.

17. See Ball, 1981; and *The Military Balance, 1982–1983.*

18. See James A. Winnefeld and Carl H. Builder, "ASW—Now or Never," *U.S. Naval Institute Proceedings* (September 1971).

19. Assumes the SS-N-18 missiles are armed with Mod 3 warheads.

20. Ball, 1981, p. 15.

21. To attack most Soviet airbases with under ten minutes warning would require forward deployment of submarines in the Mediterranean, Norwegian (or Barents), Kara (or Laptev), Japanese, and Bering seas.

22. Sanctuaries have been discussed in the literature on many occasions. See, for example, Garwin, 1972; and Joel Wit, "Sanctuaries and Security," *Arms Control Today* (October 1980).

23. See "Sailing under the Ice," *Metal Stamping, Pressing and Coating* (June 1984), pp. 121–123; "The Frozen War," *Newsweek* (January 23, 1984), pp. 36–38; and "Sub Duels Under Polar Ice: How Ready is US?" *U.S. News and World Report* (March 5, 1984), pp. 35–36.

24. A 1982 *Los Angeles Times* article reported that U.S. Navy officials believe a Soviet commando team landed by submarine on Iceland that year and cut a cable leading from a U.S. underwater acoustic array to a processing center. See Patrick Sloyan.

25. Barry R. Posen, "Inadvertent Nuclear War? Escalation and NATO's Northern Flank," *International Security* (Fall 1982), p. 36.

26. Norman Friedman, "SOSUS and U.S. ASW Tactics," *U.S. Naval Institute Proceedings* (March 1980).

27. Ibid.

8 | On–Site, Automated Monitoring: An Application for Reducing the Probability of Accidental Nuclear War

Victor A. Utgoff

MANY ARMS CONTROL ideas have foundered, at least in part, as a result of predictable limitations on the United States' capability to monitor compliance with their prospective provisions. Difficulties in verifying agreements are due primarily to three constraints on the monitoring techniques the United States is obliged to employ.

First, the Soviet Union's record in observing the provisions of past arms control treaties has been spotty, to say the least. Not surprisingly, the effect of this behavior has been to squeeze out any "benefit-of-the-doubt" the Soviet Union might have received in the past. Today, the Soviet Union is presumed guilty of violating arms control provisions until proven innocent. Thus, future arrangements for monitoring arms control agreements will have to prove continuously that the Soviets are innocent beyond any reasonable doubt. This is not necessarily a bad situation, however lamentable the events that have led to it. Nonetheless, it is an extraordinarily high standard by which to judge the "verifiability" of prospective agreements.

The second constraint on monitoring techniques is that the U.S. government is obliged to demonstrate, in a relatively open manner, its

The author is indebted to the Institute for Defense Analyses and the Defense Nuclear Agency for their permission to draw on material prepared for other purposes. The author is grateful to his colleagues at IDA who performed much of the technical work upon which this article is based, and to many others who provided helpful suggestions, but most of all to the late Mr. Joseph Beardwood, III, without whom this work would not have been done. The author bears sole responsibility, however, for this interpretation of that work.

ability to monitor compliance. While the government may be coy officially regarding specific monitoring methods, many people become familiar with their details in the course of the development, negotiation, and ratification of any treaty, and later in activities to monitor compliance with the agreement. The large numbers of people involved implies a large risk that the means of verification will be substantially compromised. Thus some monitoring techniques of particularly high intelligence value may be ruled out for arms control use.

The third general constraint on U.S. monitoring techniques is the Soviet Union's relentless effort to hold knowledge of its internal activities and foreign contacts with its citizens to a minimum. The Soviet Union believes its ability to keep its activities secret gives it an enormous advantage over the more open Western democracies. Travel of foreigners within the Soviet Union is sharply restricted; enormous areas are strictly off limits to all foreigners.

The net effect of this great concern for secrecy has been to rule out any arms control proposal that can only be monitored by means of continuous inspections by foreigners of activities inside the Soviet Union. Though on-site inspections on Soviet territory have been proposed for a variety of purposes on many occasions since at least 1958, the Soviet Union has so far conclusively accepted such a monitoring provision only in connection with the 1976 Treaty on Peaceful Nuclear Explosions. This agreement provides for temporary, on-site inspection of peaceful nuclear explosions of certain specified characteristics. The significance of this single exception is limited, however, by the fact that the Soviet Union has yet to declare an intention to carry out the type of peaceful nuclear explosion that would require the agreed on-site procedures to be implemented.

Nevertheless, the Soviet Union seems to be moving slowly toward accepting the notion that cooperating in allowing some degree of on-site inspection of activities inside Soviet territory may be in its own interests. In the early 1960s, the Soviet Union proposed the use of on-site, unmanned seismic stations for monitoring a comprehensive nuclear test ban (CTB). In the late 1970s, the Soviet Union agreed in negotiations for a CTB, in principle, to the emplacement of ten such stations on its territory. Recently, the Soviet Union has suggested it could agree to on-site inspections to verify the destruction of declared stocks of chemical warfare munitions. While no procedures for inspections on Soviet territory have so far been completely agreed on and implemented, on-site inspection appears nonetheless to be the most promising avenue for significant movement in arms control monitoring capabilities.

The Soviet Union's relatively forthcoming attitude toward unmanned seismic stations is particularly interesting in this connection. It raises the possibility that the Soviet Union might find it reasonable to accept other types of on-site, automated sensor systems on its territory. Such systems could conceivably perform a variety of tasks, from monitoring specific types of agreements to gathering and processing information for confidence-building measures.

In this paper, I describe the general functions any automated on-site monitoring system must be capable of carrying out. I then describe in some detail a particular application of such a system. This application would have the United States and the Soviet Union deploy automated radar stations in each other's territory to verify when silo-based intercontinental ballistic missiles (ICBMs) have not been launched. The objective of this application would be to provide a highly reliable early counter to a false indication of an ICBM attack originating from current launch detection systems. Higher reliability for both sides' attack warning systems, particularly in crises, could help to further reduce the probability of accidental nuclear war. Finally, the paper briefly discusses several other applications of automated on-site monitoring.

FUNCTIONAL REQUIREMENTS AND GENERAL PROPERTIES OF ON-SITE, AUTOMATED MONITORING SYSTEMS

There are three general functions any automated on-site sensor system must carry out. First, it must employ a sensor, or combination of sensors, to reliably detect, and in some cases measure, the important characteristics of the events to be monitored. Second, the system must be designed to communicate back to its owner whatever information is needed to meet its objectives. In some cases these communications would have to be immediate and continuous; in others the information of interest may be recorded for later collection.

Third, the system must be protected against covert tampering. Specifically, provisions must be made to detect and recognize any attempts to alter the internal functioning of the system's components, to block its intended access to the events to be detected or measured, or to substitute false communications signals for those generated by the

monitoring system. In most cases, guarding against counterfeit communications signals will require that the monitoring system "authenticate" its communications by encoding them in some way that
the host country cannot independently duplicate.

In addition, to maximize the acceptability of any on-site automated
monitoring system, it should have the following general properties:

First, the system must be designed to perform an important arms
control or confidence-building function. Neither side would be willing to go to the trouble of negotiating and implementing monitoring
procedures simply to demonstrate that such arrangements were feasible politically and technically.

Second, if the United States is to depend upon an on-site, automated
monitoring system to carry out any truly important function, it must
be extremely reliable. Great reliability is also needed if a requirement to
visit the monitors frequently for repairs is to be avoided; any such
requirements could cast doubt on the claim that the system was unmanned.

Third, the monitoring system should report back to its owners only
the minimum amount of information necessary to perform its designated function. It may have to collect a great deal of information to
perform this function, but these data should be processed on-site as
much as possible and only answers to specific questions sent back to the
owner's country. For example, a system intended to monitor the
continued absence of nuclear weapons from a particular area would
have to make continuous measurements of various kinds of radiation.
In reporting home, however, the system need only answer a question
such as this: Have you detected levels of nuclear radiation greater than
twice the normal background levels in the last hour? The host country
would be permitted to verify that only the answers to such questions
were being communicated out of its territory, rather than the raw data,
which it may consider to be more sensitive. The Soviet Union should
be willing to allow the gathering of a great deal of necessary information, if this information were to be processed on-site and clearly would
be unavailable for other uses.

During the more than two decades since the Soviet Union first
proposed on-site automated monitoring devices for verification of a
comprehensive nuclear test ban, enormous progress has been made in
the technologies needed to build devices capable of performing the
general functions outlined above.

Relatively inexpensive and reliable, high-capacity, satellite-based communications systems are now available. These can provide a continuous flow of information between each country and whatever unmanned monitors it had deployed inside the territory of the other. Similarly, enormous progress has been made in the development of small, sensitive, reliable, and inexpensive sensors of various kinds, such as radars, seismometers, acoustic devices, and infrared radiation detectors.

The most significant progress, however, has been made in the development of small, inexpensive, and reliable minicomputers and powerful software to go with them. Appropriately designed minicomputers can make use of sophisticated pattern-recognition algorithms to process enormous amounts of data quickly and come to reliable conclusions as to whether prohibited activities are taking place. By such "filtering" of the possibly sensitive raw data at the sensor site itself, the difference between the Soviet Union's concerns with U.S. "spying" and the U.S. requirements for sufficient information to allow reliable verification of arms control agreements may be bridged.

Finally, the past two decades have witnessed the development of small, reliable, and inexpensive encryption devices that can be used to authenticate communications between the unmanned monitoring devices and their owners, thus assuring each side that the other is not masking illegal activities by deceiving the detection device and substituting doctored information for authentic monitoring data.

Progress in these various areas has been due primarily to developments in electronics, beginning with the invention of the transistor and progressing through integrated circuits of extremely small-size and low-power requirements. These developments have been the basis for some very sophisticated automated systems, from autopilots capable of making completely unmanned landings of air and spacecraft, to complex assembly lines worked solely by robotic machine tools. In fact, the concept we are suggesting here can be restated as a design for "monitoring robots."

One might expect the Soviet Union to find robots far more acceptable for on-site monitoring purposes than human beings. Robots behave far more predictably than human beings. Their capabilities can be limited and completely understood. Robots are not going to attempt to subvert the citizens of their host country. Robots seem far less intrusive inhabitants of areas near important Soviet activities than human beings.

Robots are also hopeless targets for bribery attempts. They are likely to be less expensive to maintain. They don't need vacations. Robots don't get bored and inattentive. In many ways robots would seem superior to human beings for some kinds of monitoring tasks.

A SPECIFIC APPLICATION

As stated earlier, automated on-site monitoring schemes have been proposed in the past, but never implemented. In considering alternative applications of this concept that might have better prospects of being implemented, it seems wise to start with an application that is simple and minimally intrusive. The author proposed a study of such an application to the Defense Nuclear Agency and received support for an examination of its feasibility. The results of that study are summarized in the following text. The reader should appreciate that the monitoring system discussed in this paper takes advantage of a number of ideas developed for the unmanned seismic sensor system that was intended to help monitor a comprehensive nuclear test ban.

Objective

The objective of this application of robot monitoring would be to reduce the probability of accidental nuclear war, in particular a war resulting from one side receiving a false indication of a large-scale launch of the other side's intercontinental ballistic missiles and immediately launching its own nuclear forces as a result. This kind of accident is admittedly very unlikely. The United States deploys infrared sensors on satellites that can detect the exhaust plumes of ballistic missiles as they boost their way out of the lower atmosphere. The Soviet Union is reported to have deployed similar warning satellites. Both sides have deployed radar warning systems on the earth's surface that can detect missiles as they come over the horizon on the final portions of their attack trajectories. Satellite-based detection systems would provide warning of an attack within one or two minutes of a large-scale ICBM launch; ground-based radar warning systems would provide corroboration fifteen to twenty minutes later.

While we know very little regarding the reliability of the Soviet Union's warning systems, our own systems produce false indications of large-scale attacks very rarely. On the few occasions when they have given such false warnings, cross-checks between the two types of warning systems, double-checks of the raw data being received, and examinations of the system for other possible explanations of the indications of attack have led to an understanding that the attack indication was a false one within a few minutes.

In addition, the few instances of false warning of a large attack that have occurred have all taken place in a relatively peaceful international environment. In the absence of other signs of the many preparations we would expect the Soviet Union to take before starting a nuclear war, responsible U.S. officials would be skeptical of an indication of a large-scale attack and, correspondingly, would spend a few extra minutes cross-checking the warning data before considering concrete preparations for retaliation.

Both sides are improving their current attack warning systems, and these improvements should further reduce the probability of false indications of a large-scale attack. While this general situation should be the source of considerable confidence that the kind of accident postulated here were extremely unlikely, there are some good reasons to remain concerned and to consider further improvements in the reliability of both sides' warning systems, assuming that they could be implemented at reasonable cost.

First and foremost, the costs of an accidental nuclear war could be so great that even marginal reductions in the already low probability of such an accident are worth serious consideration. Second, as the Soviet Union continues to deploy ICBMs that are capable of destroying the silos housing U.S. ICBMs, and as the United States improves the accuracy of its Minuteman ICBMs and moves to deploy the new MX missile in silos, the context for interpreting false warnings of ICBM attacks is getting more dangerous. In future crises, the fact that each side's nonmobile missiles would be vulnerable to attack is bound to make both nations extremely nervous. Each would worry about the possibility that the other side may be tempted to seek the military advantages of a successful preemptive attack against the other's vulnerable forces.

Finally, however confident the United States may be regarding the reliability of its own attack warning systems, it does not know how reliable the Soviet Union's warning systems may be. It is known that the United States has significant advantages over the Soviet Union in some of the technologies upon which the current attack warning systems are based. It is also known that Soviet military doctrine calls for launching nuclear retaliatory strikes against the West when the Soviet Union detects signs that the United States is preparing to launch an attack. These observations suggest it is in the United States' interest to consider ways to improve the Soviet Union's missile attack warning capabilities and to build Soviet confidence in the effective functioning of their system.

The Concept

To further improve the reliability of each side's overall attack warning system, the two nations could agree to install automated monitoring systems capable of detecting missile launches near each other's ICBM deployment areas. These monitors would communicate the absence of such launches back to their owner's country continuously. They would be designed to detect and report any attempt to tamper with them.

Adding this new attack warning system would raise the number of attack warning systems on each side from two to three, a value in itself. More importantly, adding this new system would create the possibility of cross-checking attack indications between two sensor systems within no more than one to two minutes of the suspected launching of an attack. This would compare very favorably with the cross-check delay of the current pairs of sensor systems, which can run as high as ten minutes or more.

Note that this new system would be different in two important ways from the attack warning systems already in existence. First, it would carry out its detections locally, from distances on the order of tens of miles, rather than from distances of thousands of miles, as is the case with the current systems. This means that the missile sensing techniques it would employ need not be nearly as sophisticated as those employed by the current warning systems. Second, since the proposed system would be located on the sovereign territory of the host nation, it would function only as a cooperative measure. It would be there to help verify that the host nation had not launched an ICBM attack, so long as the host nation wished to make such verification feasible. The system could not be counted on to provide any assistance in the case of an intended, rather than accidental, nuclear war. The implications of this observation are explored in more depth in the text that follows.

Alternative Sensors

We assume that neither the United States nor the Soviet Union would want the other to be able to get so close to its missile silos as to allow really elementary solutions to the problem of detecting missile launches, such as wiring silo doors to detect their opening. Neither side would want to permit the other such close observation of its missile facilities and operations as the installation, operation, and maintenance of any such system inevitably would require. Moreover, a detection system located some distance away could remain out of sight and thus constitute a less salient reminder of a foreign presence. Further, if the system could be located where people and machines need not approach it, its environment would be less noisy and guarding the device against tampering would be less difficult.

We therefore examined a number of alternative sensors for the purpose of detecting missile launches at ranges between a few kilometers and many tens of kilometers. Detailed studies were carried out of infrared sensors to detect the heat of missile exhausts, seismic and acoustic sensors to detect the pressure waves generated by missile firings and transmitted through the air or ground, high-frequency electromagnetic energy detectors to sense the atmospheric ionization generated by missile exhausts, and microwave radar detectors.

A microwave radar system appears best for this application. The technology of microwave radars is relatively mature and reliable radars can be built at low cost. A single radar can detect missile launches from anywhere within any current missile deployment area in the United States and the Soviet Union.

How the Radar Would Function

One radar system would monitor each field of missile silos from a distance of fifty to sixty kilometers down range toward its owner's country. The radar system would employ a fixed antenna to stare straight upward through a minimum volume of space encompassing all the potential trajectories from the missile field it would be guarding to points within the continental territory of the other side (see Figure 8-1).

The radar would be designed to detect single missile launches with a high probability and multiple launches with a very high probability. The probability that it would miss any single missile launch would be less than one in a hundred. The probability of missing a multiple launch involving at least five distinct missile trajectories would be less than one in a billion. Multiple launches, of course, are of the greater interest, since hundreds of missiles would be required for a militarily meaningful first strike.

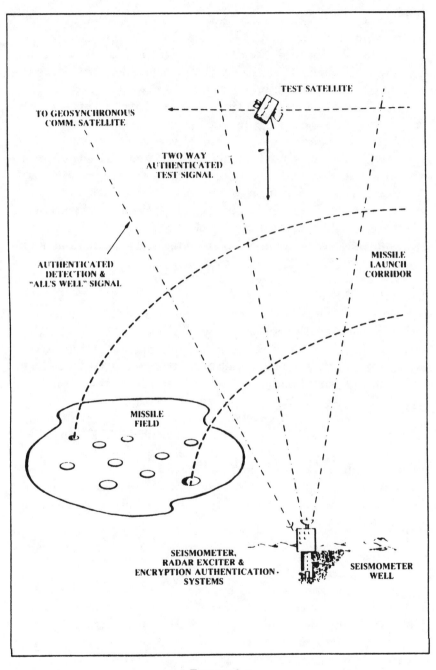

FIGURE 8-1

The radars must generate very few false alarms if they are to make the maximum contribution to reducing the overall probability of a false alarm. As designed, the combined system of radars needed to monitor all the Soviet Union's ICBM fields would generate a false alarm of a single missile launch on the average of once every six months. More important, false alarms of an attack involving a sufficient number of missiles to place U.S. silo-based ICBM forces in jeopardy would occur with a frequency of less than one every 10,000 years.

Finally, the radar would be designed to filter out all signals except those exhibiting the range and velocity profiles of missile trajectories, or those that might result from an attempt to block the radars' "vision" of the volume of space within which it is supposed to detect missiles. (This point will be revisited later.) The purpose of this filtering is to help limit the information gathered by the radar to the minimum required to perform its required functions.

Communications

Since the purpose of these radar monitors is to provide continuous verification that an ICBM attack has not been launched (when that is the case), the radars must be in continuous communication with their owner's country. Each radar installation would be provided therefore with a satellite communications link. The radar monitors inside the Soviet Union would relay their communications up to a commercial satellite parked at geosynchronous altitude over the Indian Ocean, thence down to the transceiving station at Goonhilly, U.K., up to the geosynchronous relay satellite over the mid-Atlantic, and then down to appropriate locations in the United States. Arrangements would have to be made to ensure that these communications were never bumped for other traffic employing these same links, such as video relay of soccer games.

Tamper Proofing

If any significant use is to be made of the information provided by these radar monitors, they must be designed so as to ensure that they could not be tampered with in a manner that would not be detected immediately. As noted earlier, three distinct approaches to tampering must be guarded against.

First, in order to guard against attempts to tamper with the internal workings of the radar monitors, we would agree with the Soviet

Union that they were not to be approached, except in the company of representatives of the other side. To verify compliance with this agreement, the installations would be fenced off and instrumented to detect any attempted approaches.

The main detection system used for this purpose would be a very sensitive seismometer located in a deep well beneath the installation. Short-range acoustic and infrared sensors could also be used to detect approaches to the installation. Internal voltages, temperatures, wind speeds, light intensities, and other physical parameters could be monitored. A computer inside each installation would compare these measurements with a set of acceptable values recorded in its memory. Deviations from acceptable limits would be communicated immediately to the owner nation. The one exception to this "filtering" arrangement would be the information from the seismometer, which would be sent out unprocessed. Reasons for this exception will be made clear shortly.

To guard against any attempt to block the radar's ability to see through the volume of space it was supposed to monitor, two means would be employed.

First, the radar filters would be designed to allow detection and reporting of any signals of the type that would be created by radar pulses reflected from any blocking surface that was interposed between the radar and potential missile trajectories. We assume that any blocking surface would be designed to reflect energy away from the return path to the radar and/or absorb it. It can be demonstrated that even if such a reflector/absorber surface were capable of reflecting back toward the radar as little as 1/100,000th of the radar energy impinging upon it (a spectacular technical breakthrough in itself), detection of the blocking surface would be ensured, unless the surface were interposed at an altitude of tens of kilometers above the radar. In this case, the surface would have to be several kilometers long. Even if such a surface could be constructed, it would be extremely bulky and would take considerable time to move into position. Further, it would likely be visible through national technical means.

As a second check that the radar could see through the space it is supposed to monitor, test satellites utilizing a radar transponder to carry on a "conversation" with the radar installations while passing overhead would be employed. The system design employs four satellites in polar orbits, which allows a check of each installation every three hours. While overhead, the test satellites would interrogate each installation and record its answer for later relay to a ground station when passing over the owner's country. The radar installations would send back to the owner's country the interrogating signal immediately upon receipt, over their own satellite communications links. This would make it clear that the test systems were working.

Finally, to guard against substitution of counterfeit communications that would indicate that all is well, when the radars were being tampered with or missiles were being launched, all communications would be authenticated with encryption devices. These devices would be located in the seismometer wells under each radar installation and aboard each of the test satellites.

The encryption devices would be employed to derive from each block of communicated data, and then append to that block, several additional "authentication bits" of signal. The devices must ensure that the correspondence between the data and the authentication bits cannot be puzzled out. To ensure this, the transmitted data must have an enormous number of possible values to defeat any attempt to build a "library" of data blocks and corresponding authentication bits. Sending back the raw seismometer data would suit this purpose admirably.

The interrogation signals sent by the test satellites would be generated by the ground station in the owner's country as each satellite moves toward its next pass over the host country. These signals could be made as complex as necessary to defeat attempts at cataloging. Authentication devices suitable to these requirements were built and certified as safe for this kind of application by the U.S. government as part of the development of devices to monitor a comprehensive test ban.

While these techniques should ensure that the radar monitoring system could not be tampered with covertly, construction and test of such devices might reveal other possibilities that would have to be guarded against. As part of any implementation of this radar monitoring scheme, therefore, a "red team" effort should be maintained to look for ways to subvert the system.

Collateral Values
There are a number of potential collateral values that the United States might realize by negotiating and implementing an agreement to install radar monitors on U.S. and Soviet territory.

First, the existence of such monitors could provide strategic warning that the USSR were preparing for an attack. In the event they initiated a deliberate attack, the Soviet Union would not want the United States to have the extra tactical warning the monitors would provide. Thus, the USSR would want to shut them down in advance of any such attack. No doubt some pretext could be found, such as a claim that the installations had been discovered to be spying on the Soviet Union by some previously hidden means. Regardless of the pretext, however, any shutdown of our monitors would provide strategic warning of a possible attack.

Second, because the monitors necessarily would improve each side's warning of attack in one way or the other, by agreeing to install such monitors the United States and the Soviet Union would provide each other with additional assurance that neither intended to attempt a disarming attack against the other. Thus, implementation of this monitoring scheme could not only add to stability in a crisis, but also could have a small, but steady, tempering effect on day-to-day relations between the two great powers. If the Soviet Union were to refuse a proposal to negotiate this radar monitoring scheme, by suggesting it the United States would nonetheless be providing additional assurance of its responsible attitude toward nuclear war, a factor likely to be welcomed by U.S. allies in Europe and elsewhere.

Third, implementation of this scheme for automated on-site monitoring would set a very valuable precedent for a wide range of potential arms control agreements. By negotiating and implementing this minimally intrusive, on-site monitoring scheme, both sides would also gain valuable experience that might encourage consideration of other forms of automated on-site monitoring.

Fourth, implementation of this proposal might help to rally domestic political support for negotiated measures of arms control. For a variety of reasons, progress in arms control has come only very slowly in recent years. This has led to significant domestic support for more radical arms control proposals, some of which may not be in the best interest of the U.S., and even some support for measures involving a degree of unilateral disarmament. Successful negotiation on the practical type of agreement described in this paper could provide encouragement to advocates of negotiated arms control, particularly given its precedent-setting nature, and could reduce the pressures for less desirable arms control measures.

Finally, we should emphasize again that given its design, we could expect to gain only negligible intelligence from these devices, aside from that inherent in their stated monitoring function. Even if the radar installations were allowed to remain functioning during a limited ICBM attack, they are designed with relatively low resolution. Thus, they could not be used to backtrack the missile trajectories they observe in order to gain information on which missile silos remain loaded, and this would be their most obvious potential intelligence function.

Conceivable Problems and Limitations

Three significant potential problems and limitations to this automated monitoring concept were identified in the course of the study. First, proposing to negotiate an agreement of this kind would inevitably highlight the question of accidental nuclear war. Given the growing public concern regarding the possible consequences of a large-scale nuclear war and the growth in numbers of nuclear warheads during the last decade, drawing attention to the possibilities of accidental war might increase pressures for unilateral arms control measures that were not in the U.S. interest. Alternatively, it may be that the public's awareness of the possibilities and consequences of accidental nuclear war is already so high, as a result of coverage of the subject in various media, that this reminder would have only negligible effects of this kind. If this were the case, the net public reaction may simply be to applaud this attempt to reduce the chances of accidental nuclear war even further.

Second, the Soviet Union would undoubtedly insist on receiving exact copies of any monitoring device to be installed in its territory. Provisions to this effect cover any equipment to be installed on-site for monitoring large peaceful nuclear explosions, and also were agreed to in the course of negotiations on the CTB. The Soviet Union's purpose in wanting these samples of equipment is to test and tear them down, in order to assure themselves that the equipment is only capable of performing its agreed functions. Given the Soviet Union's insistence on such provisions, the United States could not utilize equipment that incorporated technology that would contribute to Soviet military capabilities or that would compromise significant U.S. technological advantages. As designed, however, the radar monitors include only technologies that we know the Soviet Union already has or that were included in the on-site monitoring stations the United States intended to give to the Soviet Union under the CTB.

Finally, one might argue that automated on-site monitoring of ICBMs will become less important as both sides deploy submarine-launched ballistic missiles and mobile ICBMs with the accuracies and yields required to destroy hard targets. This is true to some extent, but several points should be kept in mind. First, it will be a long time before the United States and the Soviet Union deploy sufficient numbers of these other systems to threaten the destruction of either side's silo-based ICBM force. Second, even after such deployments have taken place, the monitors would still be important to confirm that a side had not launched its ICBMs. Despite the possible presence of alternative weapons capable of destroying hard targets, each side may expect a large ICBM launch to be the lead element of any preemptive strike by the other side, since these forces could not be expected to survive retaliation anyway. In any case, unless other U.S. and Soviet warning systems reached the sublime state of perfect reliability, the possibility for a false indication of an ICBM attack would continue to exist no matter what other forces may have been deployed. The radar monitors would thus continue to perform a useful function in helping to deny that falsely indicated launches of fixed ICBMs were real.

Costs

Cost estimates were developed for the system of radar monitors described in this paper. All of the individual components of the system, or very similar components, have been manufactured recently in the United States. The cost of the individual radar monitoring installations was thus estimated as the sum of appropriately adjusted costs of these components, plus an estimate of integration and check-out costs. An estimate of the start-up cost of the overall monitoring system was then derived by summing the costs of a sufficient number of radar monitors, together with items such as transport and installation of the monitors, an initial set of test satellites, launch of these satellites, a control station in the United States, and maintenance manuals. We included cost estimates for every start-up cost we could imagine, with the result of a one-time outlay of roughly $60 million (at 1983 prices).

In constructing an estimate of the continuing costs to the United States of operating the system of monitoring stations in the Soviet Union, we assumed that the entire system would have to be replaced every four years. This replacement cost estimate was summed with estimated costs for items such as pay and allowances for control station and field maintenance crews, maintenance crew travel, use of the required commercial satellite links, a small "red team" effort to continuously search for ways the system could be subverted, and escorts for Soviet personnel on maintenance visits to their stations. We again included cost estimates for every continuing cost we could imagine, which resulted in a yearly cost of roughly $12 million (at 1983 prices).

We did not attempt to construct a cost estimate for an analogous set of automated monitors for operation in the United States by the Soviet Union. If the Soviet Union were to employ a system of similar design, its costs should be somewhat lower than ours, because the United States has fewer ICBM deployment areas than does the Soviet Union.

It is of course a matter of judgment as to whether these costs are too high a price to pay for the collection of potential benefits and limitations that might be realized from implementing this on-site monitoring scheme. To place these costs in perspective, however, we note that the total cost to the United States of setting up this monitoring system and operating it for ten years would be less than 5 percent of the total amount we will spend during the 1980s on the current two ICBM attack warning systems.

GENERALIZATION OF THE AUTOMATED ON-SITE MONITORING CONCEPT

Other potential applications of automated on-site monitoring are conceivable. For example, it might prove possible to monitor an agreement to keep missile launchers outside an agreed prohibited area. This might be done using small tamper-proof boxes welded to each launcher and capable of receiving signals sent out by the U.S. system of global positioning satellites. The boxes would use these signals to compute an answer to the question: Are you inside the prohibited area? The answer, plus information on the "state of health" of the monitor, would be authenticated and, by untraceable means, periodically relayed by the host back to a central collection point, and from there back to the monitoring country.

Another potential application might monitor the numbers of missiles deployed in a multiple shelter basing scheme. Each shelter would be monitored by a tamper-proof system that could determine whether that shelter were occupied by a missile. The monitoring signals from each shelter would be authenticated and relayed to a central collection point where the total number of occupied shelters would be calculated. Only this total would be sent back to the monitoring country. This would allow verification of the number of missiles deployed overall without allowing determination of which shelters were occupied.

Determination of whether these potential applications of the general concept of automated on-site robot monitoring would prove technically feasible and affordable would require considerable further analysis. For that matter, the need for and acceptability of these specific types of monitoring arrangements is far from clear. Both these examples are more intrusive than the on-site automated ICBM launch monitors described earlier.

Nonetheless, this general approach to loosening the current constraints on on-site monitoring deserves careful attention. If some imaginative souls across the United States were given support for a vigorous search for other applications, there is no telling what they might produce.

9 | Expanding the U.S.–USSR Military Dialogue

Wade J. Williams

The United States has more to fear from them [the Soviets] *not* understanding than understanding us.''[1]

THE ABOVE STATEMENT by McGeorge Bundy, National
Security Advisor to Presidents Kennedy and Johnson, encapsulates a
general feeling regarding relations between the United States and the
Soviet Union. Close allies during the victorious campaign against Nazi
Germany in World War II, the termination of hostilities found the
United States and Soviet Union the two most powerful military
powers on earth. But the cooperation of World War II and its attendant
euphoria were fleeting. Soviet backing of Communist insurgent forces
in Greece, Soviet pressures on Turkey to cede territory and make other
concessions, Soviet intransigence regarding Iran, the continued
occupation of nations in Eastern Europe and Soviet subversion of
noncommunist governments there, and, finally, the acquisition of
atomic and thermonuclear weapons by the USSR all led to the "cold
war." Popular hopes for global peace, solution of the world's problems by the members of the United Nations Security Council, and a
future noted more by cooperation than confrontation were short lived.
The Berlin crises of 1948 and 1961; Korea; uprisings in Eastern Europe,

This research paper, written while the author was a student at the National War College,
represents the views of the author and does not necessarily reflect the official opinion of the
National War College, the National Defense University, the Department of Defense, or
other agencies of the Federal Government.

Vietnam, and Afghanistan are all now chapters in an unfinished saga. And throughout this entire post–World War II period there has been a threat of direct military hostilities between the two great powers with an attendant risk of escalation to nuclear war.

The basic differences between the United States, with its emphasis on individual liberties, freedom of expression, and a free-market economy, and the Soviet Union, which advocates subservience of the individual to the state, state control of all means of communication, and a socialist economy, are deep and profound. In the past, such significant differences in all likelihood would have led to military conflict. But in present circumstances, the United States and the Soviet Union both seem to understand that war between them would probably have no "victor," certainly not if it resulted in a nuclear exchange. Even so, the possibility of a war between the great powers cannot be ruled out since neither nation trusts the other and both have global political, economic, and security interests which, in most cases, are diametrically opposed.

This paper is predicated on the assumption that in the foreseeable future neither nation will change the major components of its basic philosophy or its resultant foreign policy. Military arsenals will remain an irreducible component in the pursuit of each nation's goals and, although each nation's political and economic aims will take precedence, military confrontation cannot be ruled out if one or the other perceives that its most vital interests are threatened.

The problem, then, is how each nation defines its own national interests and how it perceives those of its antagonist. The process involves political leaders making political decisions. But those political decisions must be influenced by military advice based upon the best information available to military leaders. Both nations possess impressive intelligence collection capabilities which can report elaborately on the other's *capabilities*, but they have a far more difficult problem discerning each other's *intentions*. Yet, during times of heightened tensions or actual crises, such perceptions of intentions may be the final determinant of decisions. By helping to ensure that more accurate perceptions are formed, an expanded military dialogue between the two sides, developed slowly over a considerable period of time, may help to defuse potentially dangerous encounters.[2]

With this perspective as a starting point, the author interviewed nearly twenty individuals with backgrounds as military commanders, chiefs of military intelligence agencies, arms control negotiators, or academicians. The aim of the interviews was to elicit the personal experience of these experts in dealing with the Soviet military and their views on how best to deal with the Soviet Union. Based on this information, I discuss the practicality of an expanded U.S.–Soviet military dialogue, potential topics for discussion, possible pitfalls and drawbacks, and the relationship of any military dialogue to the governing political climate. In conclusion, I suggest specifically the type of dialogue which might be pursued most effectively.

BACKGROUND

The concept of a dialogue is neither complex nor mysterious: It is a conversation between two or more persons or an exchange of ideas and opinions. An unbroken formal, diplomatic dialogue has been maintained by the United States and the Soviet Union since 1933. Obviously, there have been ups and downs in this relationship, but both countries have found it in their interest to maintain, even in the worst of times, this channel of communications.

There also has been a certain amount of military-to-military dialogue between the United States and the USSR since the end of World War II. Information presented in Appendix 9-1, which has been provided by the staff of the Joint Chiefs of Staff, summarizes these U.S.–Soviet military exchanges and visits. Such military exchanges have been influenced heavily by the political climate. There have been no meetings of the U.S. Secretary of Defense and the Soviet Minister of Defense in the postwar era, although such visits were proposed during both the Nixon and the Carter administrations. The Soviet Union has not yet responded to Secretary of Defense Harold Brown's proposal of such an exchange in 1979, and with the subsequent deterioration of bilateral relations the prospects are not sanguine. Similarly, there have been no visits involving the Chairman of the Joint Chiefs of Staff and his Soviet counterpart—the Chief of the General Staff. Although the possibility of such a meeting was raised initially in 1956 and Chairman David Jones did meet informally with Marshall Ogarkov at the Vienna Summit in 1979, the Soviet invasion of Afghanistan has stifled further movement at this level.

One service chief, Air Force Chief of Staff General Nathan F. Twining, did visit the Soviet Union in 1956 as a guest of the then Defense

Minister, Marshal of the Soviet Union, Zhukov. Soviet military representatives periodically have reminded U.S. Embassy personnel in informal conversations in Moscow that no reciprocal visit has taken place. Finally, the possibility of the exchange visit of several U.S. Army general officers to Moscow in 1978, to have been followed by an Air Force exchange in 1979, showed great promise of reaching fruition, but was never implemented as a result of Soviet activities in the Horn of Africa. The Soviets still view the U.S. decision to cancel those planned exchanges as precipitous and have now adopted a "ball-is-in-your court" attitude, asserting that the United States should make the next move.

There have been some encouraging exchanges of military personnel at lower levels. There have been periodic contacts between the Commander-in-Chief of the U.S. Army in Europe, for example, and his Soviet counterpart. As noted in interviews with four previously high-ranking U.S. Army officials in Europe (Generals Davison, Blanchard, Kroessen, and Goodpaster), these contacts and visits, although certainly not seminal regarding their impact on U.S.–Soviet relations, have provided an opportunity to catch a glimpse of Soviet military thinking and outlook. They also suggest the possibility of providing a conduit or setting for expanded contacts in the future. The 1970s also witnessed successful exchanges of military historians, military college students, military lecturers, port visits by warships, and regular contacts between U.S. and Soviet naval delegations in conjunction with yearly meetings about incidents at sea.

As the foregoing illustrates, the idea of a Soviet–U.S. military dialogue is not a new or revolutionary idea. Discounting the "Incidents at Sea" Agreement, however, nothing concrete or permanent has been established. It is obvious that military contact has reflected the temper of the political climate and will undoubtedly continue to do so in the future. But even while the political tide ebbs and flows, the danger of military confrontation will be present for both nations. And as President Reagan has pointed out recently, the military in the Soviet Union may be playing a larger role in Soviet policymaking:

> There is one new development that I have worried about for some time—that is the extent, lately, to which military leaders in the Soviet Union are, apparently without any coaching or being briefed by the civilian part of government—at least there is no evidence of that—taking it upon themselves to make statements, and rather bellicose statements. There has not, in the

past, been evidence of top military leaders going public with attacks on the
U.S. and seeming to enunciate policy on their own. We have to be aware of
this and pay a little attention to this, to see if they have become a power of their
own.[3]

If President Reagan's observation is accurate, it adds a somewhat
new dimension to consider in U.S. relations with the Soviet Union.
Attention to widening contacts between U.S. military officals and
their Soviet counterparts might be considered as one possible method
of determining just how deeply the influence of the Soviet military is
felt at the highest levels of the Soviet government and just what the
perspective which they bring to bear on international problems
might be.

LESSONS OF THE PAST

To say that military contacts, exchanges, and visits between the United
States and the Soviet Union should be expanded is somewhat of a
"motherhood" statement—no one is really against it. But is it practical? And what benefit would accrue to the United States from pur-
suing such activities? In an attempt to determine answers or elicit
suggestions concerning these basic questions, a series of interviews
was conducted with individuals who have had, or still have, positions
which involve command of forces directly confronting the Soviets,
service in the American Embassy in Moscow, key intelligence or
policymaking positions, or expertise as students of the Soviet military.
The list of interviewees (see Appendix 9-2) is certainly not comprehensive, but reflects an effort to contact those individuals who were
available and knowledgeable.

The composition of the group of interviewees is heavily slanted, by
design, toward military officers. The rationale is simple. If individuals
who have spent most of their careers learning about and actually
confronting the Soviet military threat can see some thread of practicality in discussing problems or topics of mutual concern with their
Soviet counterparts, then others without similar experience, but with a
deep appreciation of the military prowess of the Soviet Union, may
take note. It is one thing to have studied the potential of the Soviet
Union's military machine from a textbook and quite another to have
commanded hundreds of thousands of troops who might have to
engage in combat with Soviet forces.

The following questions were discussed during the interviews:

Practicality of an expanded dialogue
Topics and level of discussion
Confidence-building measures
Dealing with the allies
Pitfalls and drawbacks of an expanded dialogue.

The results of these discussions are presented in the following text.

PRACTICALITY OF AN EXPANDED DIALOGUE

The aim and rationale for a broad approach to a military dialogue was stated recently by National Security Advisor Robert McFarlane, "If we can engender a kind of dialogue with the Soviets in which we make clear that this renewed sense of purpose, strength and resolve is not oriented against their system, and that we are not seeking to alter it, then this dialogue can lead to a stable *modus vivendi*. We seek that."[4]

Although every interviewee emphasized that military contacts must be conducted in light of broad political guidelines, all but one were optimistic regarding the accrual of possible benefits over drawbacks. General Goodpaster saw "great potential benefits" and a method to "cool down military confrontation." He noted further that it is to our benefit to have Soviet tactical commanders visit our units in the field and actually see our combat equipment. His personal experiences suggested that actually viewing our troops and equipment greatly impressed Soviet commanders with U.S. technological capabilities. A return visit to Soviet units would be desirable, he thought, but if it should occur, be cautioned, we should not raise our expectations too high as to what would be shown. It would be desirable to visit actual units, but just as important, General Goodpaster stated, would be the opportunity for opposing field commanders to meet, size one another up, and gain a mutual appreciation of the other's views on any of a number of military or political topics.

Three former commanders of the U.S. Army in Europe (Generals Davison, Blanchard, and Kroessen) felt that meetings between general officers of U.S. and Soviet forces in Germany should be encouraged. General Davison stated that "it adds to our perspective and provides an insight into the Soviet mind set and attitudes." General David Jones, former Chairman of the Joint Chiefs of Staff, was encouraged by his brief meeting with Marshals Ustinov and Ogarkov in 1979 in Vienna and viewed contact at all levels as a means of reducing tension and increasing understanding. McGeorge Bundy saw no reason to expect that we would lose anything by an increased military dialogue and felt that it would be to the advantage of both sides to find ways of talking.

All of the individuals contacted, except one, felt that an expanded military dialogue would be advantageous. The one exception, although not opposed to an increased dialogue per se, felt that it would be far more beneficial to get the embassy-to-embassy military relationship "straightened out first," since Soviet military representatives have far greater access in Washington than American military attachés have in Moscow. He also was wary of the "typical U.S. naiveté" in dealing with the Soviets and was of the opinion that an increased military dialogue would have nothing to do with Soviet-American relations since all relations are viewed by the Soviets in a political context, a context dictated by a combat element, the Communist party of the Soviet Union. This individual is of the view that the Soviet empire will dissolve over time and that this demise will occur earlier if contact with the West is cut off. In summary, he thought that dialogue with the Soviets is by its nature confrontational and that any contacts by the United States with the Soviets must be "under a tight leash." These candid views add a sobering light for anyone anticipating the potential benefits of an expanded dialogue.

TOPICS AND LEVEL OF DISCUSSION

Assuming that interest in a dialogue with the Soviet Union will grow, one must consider such real-life problems as what topics should be on the agenda and who should be the participants. Here we have a "chicken and egg" dilemma: Should the topics dictate the participants or vice versa? An argument can be made for either approach.

An entire range of tactical and strategic issues conceivably could be of interest. Obviously, nuclear capabilities and intentions, military uses of space, perceptions of the threats posed by each other, and such new ideas as jointly manned crisis control centers are but a few of the issues with a broad, strategic view that could be discussed. Weapon programs and other specific military activities have also been mentioned as potentially interesting. George Kennan has noted recently that those last (weapons and military activities) might very usefully include efforts to reduce the present dangerous level of aggressive military intelligence gathering, including the various forms of shadowing, snooping and spying, all of which are so pregnant with possibilities for clashes, misunderstandings and incidents. It would pay both governments to exchange certain categories of information voluntarily rather than to have them pursued by those questionable and hazardous procedures.[5]

One topic which falls into this category and has been successfully addressed by the two nations are incidents at sea involving the Navies of the United States and the Soviet Union. The Incidents at Sea Agreement, signed in 1972, enjoins the two sides to observe strictly the letter and spirit of international regulations for preventing collisions at sea, to refrain from provocative acts at sea that could increase the risk of war, and to notify mariners of actions on the high seas that represent a danger to navigation or to aircraft in flight.[6] Rear Admiral Ronald Kurth, who has a long history of involvement with both the negotiation and implementation of the Incidents at Sea Agreement, notes that the understanding "has relieved the potential for the day-to-day disasters which were present in the late 1950s and early 1960s and has led to increases in mutual understanding and confidence."[7] Experience has shown that the creation of a direct navy-to-navy channel of communications involving the service staffs and attaché personnel, in addition to yearly formal meetings, allows issues which bother, or conversely please, either navy to be handled expeditiously and professionally.

The Navy experience supports the proposition that where a commonality of interests is present a useful dialogue can be implemented. The topics of discussion at the "Incidents at Sea" dialogue are clearly relevant, and a workable degree of confidence has been engendered between the two sides. It can be safely asserted that while not all of either navy's doubts or suspicions about the other have been dissipated, what areas of friction do remain can be approached in a more effective and businesslike manner by individuals who have developed a working relationship. Some individuals contend that the dialogue created by the Incidents at Sea Agreement is primarily tactical in nature and unique in subject matter and does not necessarily lend itself as a model for the other military services or for the other types of issues. From a narrow viewpoint this argument may be correct, but what is significant is that a useful, mutually beneficial channel of communication has been functioning for over twelve years.

The more the interviews which were conducted, the more clearly emerged the view that, although there is a great appreciation of, and interest in, strategic and global issues, the one geographic area which may lend itself particularly to an expanded U.S.–Soviet military dialogue is the European theater. Whereas the U.S. and Soviet Navies have encountered each other on the open seas seriously only since the 1960s, the U.S. Army has confronted the Soviet Army across the Iron Curtain for nearly forty years. Although well-defined and heavily defended borders preclude the type of inadvertent encounters which characterize incidents at sea,[8] issues concerning the two sides' ground forces do arise about which there could be a mutual interest in discussions. These include, but are not limited to, philosophies of training, mutual perceptions of threat, roles and functions of each other's military missions, and reciprocal visits to units and training areas.

A channel to address these types of topics already exists—the liaison mission of the Commander-in-Chief of the U.S. Army in Europe, located in Potsdam, East Germany, and its counterpart—the Soviet Military Liaison Mission in Frankfurt, West Germany, representing the Commander-in-Chief of the Group of Soviet Forces in Germany. Established shortly after World War II, these military missions present a natural point of contact. Although the spirit of cooperation is certainly not nearly as great as was envisioned when the arrangement was instituted originally, the three or four, primarily social, meetings which take place each year involving general officers do offer a setting for the discussion of items of mutual interest. It is significant that an instrument is already in being which could be utilized for an expanded dialogue.

While almost any topic of military relevance which is felt to be of mutual importance could be raised at such meetings, issues which are highly contentious and political and which could lead to nothing but polemics and rhetoric should be avoided, particularly in the early stages. Topics like the KAL 007 incident or Afghanistan, for example, should be avoided. This is not to say that controversial issues could not be broached in the future, but in order to get movement, to establish a feeling of mutual respect and a conducive working atmosphere, it would be more realistic to start slowly. One topic which was repeatedly mentioned favorably by the interviewees was the record of U.S.–Soviet cooperation in World War II. This topic may prove to be a particularly appropriate way to begin such a dialogue, as May 1985 marks the fortieth anniversary of the Allied defeat of Nazi Germany, and Soviet participation in that victory is a tremendous source of national pride in the USSR.

Concerning the level at which any expanded U.S.–Soviet military contacts should be conducted, one school of thought posits that in order to set a proper mood and direction an initial meeting between the Chairman of the Joint Chiefs of Staff and his Soviet counterpart, the Chief of the General Staff, should be arranged—perhaps to mark the upcoming anniversary. Backers of this approach contend that the involvement of the two highest-ranking career military officers would send a clear signal that both great powers recognize the importance of a bilateral military dialogue. The agenda for such a meeting could involve exchanges on four or five topics of interest, thus setting the stage for follow-up meetings involving either the same two principals or specialists in the specific topics of mutual interest. The same argument has been made for meetings between service chiefs.

The primary potential drawback of any high-level meeting is its vulnerability to changing political circumstances, heightened expectations of some sort of significant breakthrough, and the likelihood that any such meeting would receive great public attention. A high-level military meeting as a follow-on to, or in conjunction with, a summit meeting of heads-of-state would make these problems more manageable, but it seems unproductive to hold the military dialogue hostage to the possibility of a summit meeting of political authorities.

The aforementioned fortieth anniversary of the defeat of Nazi Germany may be a particularly well-suited way to initiate the dialogue. General John Vessey, presently Chairman of the Joint Chiefs of Staff, is the only senior U.S. officer still on active duty who served in the European war. If he were selected to represent the United States at the Soviet celebration of the allied victory, it would carry great significance. If the political atmosphere were supportive, a visit by General Vessey to Moscow would present an ideal occasion to explore the possibility of establishing a more regular and intensified military-to-military dialogue.

As several interviewees noted, the substance of any high-level military meeting would not be nearly as important as the simple fact that such a meeting had in fact taken place. As one retired general pointed out, there is in Russian society a deep respect for the military profession, and there is further a Russian custom of "princes of both sides meeting, dropping their gloves and talking." Several other generals related how their Russian counterparts, especially those with World War II experience, would express emotional feelings concerning the horrors of war and the obligation of professional military officers to ensure that war between the United States and the USSR never occurs. This common feeling, shared among a diminishing number of World War II veterans on both sides who have had a chance to meet and talk with one another, provides a basis for future contacts which should be exploited. The interviewees highlighted the general opinion that although there are significant differences between the United States and the Soviet Union across a broad spectrum of subjects, there is an overriding sense that the importance of no single issue is so overwhelming that it should ever be allowed to lead to a U.S.–Soviet war.

Another suggestion to further a military dialogue would be to initiate an exchange program involving reciprocal lectures by general officers. Such a dialogue has been tried in the past. In 1977, for example, a U.S. general officer and two Soviet generals delivered lectures to each other's senior military schools, but future exchanges were put off in the worsening political atmosphere of the late 1970s. Visits of military historians of general officer rank also occurred in the late 1970s, but also are being held in abeyance at present.

Finally, one might consider a dialogue between operational commanders in Europe. For various reasons, very few meetings have occurred at the operational level. The positive aspects of the two navies' experiences in the "Incidents at Sea" talks have been touched upon; and these talks clearly involve operational matters. But what has been missing is a dialogue on ground forces doctrine and strategy—particularly as concerns Europe, the one place where the two sides' forces face each other directly. Although not extensive, there is a record of visits involving both sides' European commanders, and both military missions deal with the other literally on a daily basis. Mechanisms are in being for virtually any type of contact, from informal and social to direct meetings of the two commanders. A meeting involving the most senior commanders, subordinate corps or division commanders, or even senior staff officers would not be looked upon as unusual or signaling some significant demarche. These settings also provide the possibility for contacts between representatives of the Joint Chief of Staff or service staffs and their Soviet counterparts. As a location for the testing of the benefits or risks in intensified U.S.–

Soviet military dialogue, the setting in Central Europe has much in its favor.

RELATIONSHIP TO CONFIDENCE-BUILDING MEASURES

As mentioned previously, the practicality of an expanded U.S.–Soviet military dialogue must be viewed in terms of the prevalent political atmosphere. Additionally, any increased U.S.–Soviet military contact must also be considered in light of other negotiating initiatives. With the Fall 1983 Soviet decision to suspend nuclear arms control negotiations, and with no apparent movement developing in the talks on conventional forces in Vienna, increased attention has centered on the Conference on Disarmament in Europe, now being held in Stockholm. These negotiations, according to the chief U.S. representative, Mr. James E. Goodby, have only one task, "to reduce the risk of military confrontation in Europe by negotiating militarily significant, politically binding, and verifiable confidence-building measures to cover the whole of Europe as far east as the Urals in the Soviet Union." (Confidence-building measures have been defined by the U.S. State Department as those measures "designed to promote mutual knowledge and understanding of military forces and activities and to prevent misunderstanding or miscalculation in a crisis.")[9]

The 1975 Helsinki Accord already incorporates five confidence-building measures related to military activities in Europe: (1) prior notification of major military maneuvers (25,000 or more troops); (2) notification of smaller-scale maneuvers (less than 25,000 troops); (3) notification of major military movements; (4) exchange of observers; and (5) other measures including the exchange by invitation of military personnel and visits by military delegations.[10] The latter two by their very nature lend themselves as the starting point for an expanded dialogue. The track record of Warsaw Pact nations inviting observers to exercises and initiating personnel exchanges and visits by military delegations has not been encouraging to date, but at least a working mechanism has been agreed upon by which expanded contacts could be facilitated.

Agreed U.S.–Soviet confidence-building measures also include the highly publicized "Hot Line" Agreement, the previously discussed "Incidents at Sea" Agreement, and the "Accidents Measures Agreement" of 1971 concerning means to reduce the risk of inadvertent nuclear war. In addition, the United States has proposed to the Soviet Union that the two sides agree to notify one another in advance of ballistic missile launches and major nuclear exercises, and also to exchange data on the status of strategic forces. Interest in confidence-building measures has also been evident recently in the Congress. Senators Carl Levin of Michigan and Sam Nunn of Georgia proposed in March 1983 that U.S. and Soviet military leaders exchange visits with each other. They further stated,

> We must establish better communications between our respective military leaders to improve mutual understanding of the strategic objectives, forces, warning systems, command and control networks, decisionmaking processes, and the identities and personalities of the actual decision makers themselves. This is something that must be achieved regardless of Soviet aggressive behavior and, indeed, it is probably more important than ever because of such behavior. While the tensions and hostilities which result from such behavior cannot be avoided, the risk of miscalculation can be. It is just plain common sense to "know thine enemy" and make sure thine enemy knows you."

On May 25, 1983, fifty-six senators (including Nunn and Levin) forwarded a letter to President Reagan in which they proposed the establishment of a program of regular exchange visits between high-level U.S. and Soviet military personnel. It was noted in their letter that discussions should be broad in scope, as substantive as possible, and carried out by the military leaders themselves.

In short, there is broad-based interest in an expanded military dialogue as an integral component of a strategy to lessen the possibility of military conflict, either accidental or planned, between the United States and Soviet Union. This interest is manifested both in proposals which would require formal approval following strenuous negotiations and in more informal ideas for discussions between military officials. There is little doubt, however, that there is a set of common goals. In the long term, neither great power benefits from a continuing upward spiral of costs associated with the arms competition. In the short term, a lack of dialogue can lead to misperceptions or misinformation in any number of regions which the United States and Soviet Union both consider to be of "vital" importance. These are primarily policy issues, but they do contain military considerations and, as such, should be looked at in a broad dimension.

POSSIBLE PITFALLS AND DRAWBACKS

To suggest that an intensification of the military dialogue with the Soviet Union could take place without reference to the political atmosphere would be naive. After an expanded military dialogue had been initiated, however, and had been in operation for a period of time long enough for a certain level of confidence to have developed on both sides, the ability to conduct a meaningful dialogue might become less dependent on political vicissitudes. As Raymond Garthoff, former American Ambassador to Bulgaria and member of the first SALT delegation pointed out, "The broader problem of changing the current trend of reciprocal suspicion and hostility remains. Long standing (Soviet) advocates of détente and improved relations with the United States, some of whom I have known for many years, are now on the defensive. In Moscow this is no time to seem to be 'soft' on the Americans." Dimitry Proektor, a senior member of the Institute of World Economy and International Relations in Moscow buttressed this point by stating that "military détente cannot come about without substantial improvements in the political climate; but once military détente does begin, it can have a favorable influence on political détente."[12]

The preceding discussion places the topic of military dialogue in a broad context in relation to the governing political climate. Let us assume for the sake of argument that a mutual decision were made to conduct some type of expanded military contact. What factors from an American viewpoint should be considered and what would be their drawbacks?

1. *Publicity and the Desire for Immediate Results.* After almost forty years of varying degrees of cold war, a low profile, exploratory approach on the part of the United States would stand a far greater chance of acceptance by the Soviets than a highly publicized, media-covered assault. Gradualism, in terms of both subject matter and intensity of dialogue, is less likely to provoke Soviet suspicions. Similarly, patient efforts to establish a set of working rules are more likely to succeed than an emotionally charged campaign to achieve concrete results quickly.

2. *Disinformation and Propaganda.* There are those who feel that with rare exceptions Americans are not disciplined enough to engage in serious dialogue with Soviet counterparts and that the "naive" Amer-

icans are almost inevitably overwhelmed by disciplined, experienced Soviet negotiation. To this view, McGeorge Bundy stated bluntly, "Baloney, there is no reason to think that they are any smarter than we are."[13] There should be no doubt that the Soviets would attempt to use military-to-military contacts for disinformation and propaganda, but such attempts, if anticipated and planned for, need not be feared. A well-informed American career officer, backed by appropriate intelligence information, could see through propaganda/disinformation and act just as professionally and logically as his Soviet counterpart. Additionally, the longer any dialogue were established, and the more it were viewed as being in each other's mutual interest, the less a factor disinformation and propaganda would likely play.

3. *Tendency Toward Openness.* Anyone who has visited or lived in the Soviet Union cannot fail to be impressed with the inordinate attention paid to security throughout Soviet society. Immediately warming up to a stranger is not in the nature of Soviet citizens. In a military structure in which even pay scales are considered classified, no military facility is identified publicly, and enormous efforts are expended to publicize the Western threat to the motherland, no American should be sanguine about the prospects of immediately establishing an open channel of communication with his Soviet counterpart. As Averill Harriman, with long years of contact with the Soviets, noted:

> You cannot be friendly with the communists the way you can with the British or other Westerners. Their basic loyalties and conceptions are completely different. There is a certain point you can't go beyond because they are taught to believe that man is destined to live by the communist ideology and that we, the imperialist aggressors, are blocking it. You can talk about a man's religion up to a point and you can't go beyond it.[14]

4. *Intelligence Collection.* Another factor not to be totally dismissed is intelligence collection. The Soviet desire to collect intelligence data is almost limitless, and it is quite probable that any serious discussions, especially during their initial stages, would have a Soviet intelligence representative. But as one looks at the collection opportunities available to the Soviet Union, as compared to those for the United States in the closed Soviet society, it is quite likely that the increased travel and contact associated with an expanded military dialogue would be at least as much in the U.S. interest as in the Soviet Union's.

5. *Informing the Allies.* Any increased contact between the U.S. and Soviet armed forces is likely to be viewed by the NATO countries with a

combination of optimism, curiosity, and suspicion. It is not necessary that the NATO partners join in an increased military dialogue with the Soviet Union, but it would be prudent to keep them informed, to the degree possible, of the direction, scope, and general content of any exchanges. This is especially important during the initial phases of any effort to expand contacts.

In summary, there are clearly potential drawbacks inherent in an increased dialogue, but one must weigh the potential gain against these potential risks. As stated earlier, I am proposing a military dialogue, not military negotiations. The purpose is to lower the degree of misperception and establish a professional working relationship. If these goals could be met even partially, the interviews conducted confirmed that it would be worth the effort.

CONCLUSION

There is a growing consensus that the tone of Soviet–American rhetoric has reached such a tense level that serious dialogue is required to ensure that a sense of hopelessness is not allowed to develop in the great power relationship. The same feeling for the necessity of enhanced dialogue is echoed by U.S. allies and by increasing numbers of individuals who study and report on the state of U.S.–Soviet relations. At the same time it is also accepted that U.S.–Soviet relations require a desire by both nations to engage in a meaningful dialogue; it cannot be merely a unilateral decision by the United States. It is also generally accepted that discussions of the military dimension of regional conflicts possess some promise of helping to defuse confrontational situations. There is a history of military contact and dialogue between the United States and the Soviet Union, and there are established conduits available for attempting to expand that dialogue. Such a dialogue would complement any ongoing or anticipated series of concrete negotiations on arms control or other topics.

There are numerous potential issues of mutual military interest, ranging from the strategic to the tactical level, which could be placed on the agenda of such talks. Any dialogue should be looked at as just that, however—a dialogue, not an attempt to convince the other of his faults, to change his basic beliefs, or to gain some type of victory. There is little to lose by engaging in such a dialogue, and such contacts might contribute to a lower level of mutual misperceptions.

Soviet leaders, by their very nature, are extremely cautious and would undoubtedly be wary as to the motives behind a U.S. proposal to intensify military contacts. A gradual program is recommended, rather than an effort to obtain immediate tangible benefits. A high-level meeting involving the Chairman of the Joint Chiefs of Staff and the Chief of the Soviet General Staff might be considered, however, especially in light of General Vessey's service in the European Theater in World War II. The May Celebration in Moscow highlighting the fortieth anniversary of the success of our joint effort to defeat Nazi Germany might be the perfect venue for such a meeting. Another communications avenue worth examining is the reciprocal U.S. and Soviet military missions in Potsdam and Frankfurt. This venue would offer an established setting and regimen for military contacts, both social and operational; and any initial exploratory talks could be conducted with no fanfare.

APPENDIX 9-I   SYNOPSIS OF SIGNIFICANT U.S.-SOVIET
MILITARY-TO-MILITARY CONTACTS

1. Visits/exchanges by senior military officials
   a. Secretary of Defense–Minister of Defense
      There have been no exchanges at this level in the postwar era (with the partial exception of the 1956 visit to Moscow discussed below).
      Secretary Brown did meet Minister of Defense Ustinov on the fringes of the SALT II Summit (June 1979, in Vienna).
   b. Chairman of the JCS and Soviet Chief of General Staff
      Also, no exchanges at this level.
      General Jones and Marshal Ogarkov, however, did meet on the fringes on the SALT II Summit.
   c. Service Chiefs
      General Nathan F. Twining, then Chief of Staff of the Air Force, visited Moscow with a group of Air Force officers in June 1956. Visit was hosted by then Minister of Defense, Marshal of the Soviet Union Zhukov.
   d. Visits between the Commander-in-Chief, U.S. Army Europe, and the Commander-in-Chief, Group of Soviet Forces Germany
      Took place regularly during immediate post–WWII period; were discontinued as Cold War developed.
      The Commander-in-Chief, U.S. Army Europe, accepted the Commander-in-Chief, Group of Soviet Forces Germany, invitation for September 1973 visit.
      Return visit by the Commander-in Chief, Group of Soviet Forces Germany, took place in 1977.
   e. Contacts between U.S. Army Chief of Military History and Soviet Chief of the Institute of Military History

Began when Soviet history chief (General-Lieutenant Zhilin) invited U.S. Army Chief of Military History (BG Collins) to visit Moscow in May 1970.

Zhilin made return visit to United States in June 1971.

Two other reciprocal visits were made, the last being when Zhilin returned to the United States in April 1978.

2. Visits by military college students

   a. A ten-man (eight of them students) National War College delegation, led by NDU President, LTG Gard, visited Moscow, Leningrad, and Volgograd in April 1977.

   b. Return visit by a five-man (one student) Soviet delegation was made in September 1977.

   c. An *unofficial* trip (i.e., tourist status, *not* by invitation of Soviets) was made by NDU students in April 1983, as part of NDU field studies program. Group was led by NDU President, LTG Pustay.

3. Exchanges of port visits

   a. Two Soviet destroyers visited Boston in May 1975.

   b. Two U.S. destroyers (*Leahy* and *Tattnall*) visited Leningrad at about the same time.

4. Incidents at Sea talks

   a. Initiated for the purpose of establishing measures to prevent incidents involving U.S. and Soviet aircraft and naval vessels at sea; presently the *only* institutionalized contact we have with Soviet senior military officials.

   b. Meetings take place annually, rotating between Moscow and Washington; last talks were in Moscow in May 1982.

APPENDIX 9-2   INDIVIDUALS INTERVIEWED FOR RESEARCH

George Blanchard, General (Ret.), U.S.A.; Commander-in-Chief, U.S. Army Europe (1975–1979)

Barry Blechman, Assistant Director, U.S. Arms Control and Disarmament Agency (1977–1979)

McGeorge Bundy, National Security Advisor to Presidents Kennedy and Johnson (1961–1966)

Michael Davison, General (Ret.), U.S.A.; Commander-in-Chief, U.S. Army Europe (1971–1975)

Andrew Goodpaster, General (Ret.), U.S.A.; Supreme Allied Commander, Europe (1969–1974); Staff Secretary to President Eisenhower (1954–1961)

Charles Hamm, Major General, USAF; Defense Attaché, American Embassy, Moscow (1981–1983)

David Jones, General (Ret.), USAF; Chairman, Joint Chiefs of Staff (1978–1982)

Frederick Kroessen, General (Ret.), U.S.A.; Commander-in-Chief, U.S. Army Europe (1979–1983)

Ronald Kurth, Rear Admiral, USN; Naval Attaché, American Embassy, Moscow (1975–1977)

Richard Larkin, Major General, (Ret.), U.S.A.; Defense Attaché, American Embassy, Moscow (1977–1979); Chief of Staff (1979–1980) and Deputy Director Defense Intelligence Agency (1980–1981)

William Odom, Major General, U.S.A.; Assistant Chief of Staff, Intelligence, Headquarters, Department of the Army; Assistant Army Attaché, American Embassy, Moscow (1972–1974)

James Williams, Lieutenant General, U.S.A.; Director, Defense Intelligence Agency (1981–present)

Samuel Wilson, Lieutenant General, (Ret.), U.S.A.; Defense Attaché, American Embassy, Moscow (1971–1973); Director, Defense Intelligence Agency (1976–1977)

Resident Fellows, Institute for East/West Security Studies, New York

Austria: Dr. Heinz Vetschera
Federal Republic of Germany: Dr. Hilmar Linnenkamp
Italy: Marco De Andreis
Poland: Dr. Marek Grela
Switzerland: Dr. Paul Widmer

NOTES

1. Interview with McGeorge Bundy, December 8, 1983.

2. The subject of this article is military dialogue, not negotiation. Although a dialogue may lead to topics worthy of negotiation, it is believed that a dialogue should be pursued solely for the purpose of lessening or totally eliminating misperceptions. There is no requirement for signed documents or other agreements; a military dialogue may enhance or support negotiations, but would not be intended to replace them.

3. "An Interview with President Reagan," *Time* (January 2, 1984).

4. "They Are the Focus of Evil in the Modern World," *Time* (January 2, 1984).

5. George F. Kennan, "Reducing Tensions," *The New York Times* (January 15, 1984).

6. U.S. Department of State, Bureau of Public Affairs, *Security and Arms Control: The Search for a More Stable Peace* (Washington, 1983), p. 45.

7. Interview with Rear Admiral Ronald Kurth, Long Range Planning Staff, Headquarters, Department of the Navy; Former Naval Attaché, American Embassy, Moscow (October 25, 1983).

8. The Spring 1984 incident involving a U.S. Army helicopter which strayed across the border is an exception to this statement.

9. John Vinocur, "Mystery of Stockholm: What's on the Agenda?" *The New York Times* (January 18, 1984), p. A4.

10. *Security and Arms Control: The Search for a More Stable Peace,* p. 4.

11. "Visits Between U.S.–U.S.S.R. Military Leaders," *Congressional Record,* Vol. 129, No. 34 (March 17, 1983), p. 53218.

12. Stephen F. Larrabee and Dietrich Stobbe (ed.), *Confidence-Building Measures in Europe* (New York: Institute for East-West Security Studies, 1983), p. 97.

13. Interview with McGeorge Bundy, December 8, 1983.

14. Averill Harriman, "Observations on Negotiating," *Journal of International Affairs,* Volume 9, No. 1 (1975), pp. 3–4.

APPENDIXES

Appendix A
A Nuclear Risk Reduction System

The Interim Report of the Nunn-Warner Working Group on Nuclear Risk Reduction

With but few exceptions, the United States and the Soviet Union have been able to avoid confrontations entailing the risk of nuclear war. There are compelling reasons, however, for concern about the two nations' ability to avoid nuclear crises in the future.

The emergence of the U.S. and the U.S.S.R. at the end of the Second World War as the only two remaining great military powers virtually assured a continuing national rivalry that would dominate global politics. The fundamental antagonisms in values and objectives between the United States and the Soviet Union continue to make certain that, regardless of their common recognition of some shared interests (such as avoiding nuclear war), the relationship will remain competitive for many years to come.

The global ideological and political struggle between ourselves and the Soviet Union is superimposed on an increasingly fractious and troubled world. International and national conflicts — particularly in the Third World — offer tempting opportunities for military or political exploitation and often lead to the involvement of the great powers on opposing sides of these disputes. In certain circumstances, such interventions have the potential to escalate to nuclear confrontations.

The 1973 crisis in the Middle East vividly demonstrated how quickly, and how far, such situations can escalate. The two great powers' involvement began with emergency transfers of weapons, shifted rapidly to the use of their own air and naval forces to protect those shipments, and ended with mutual threats of direct military intervention to protect their respective clients. At the height of the crisis, there were even hints that such interventions might include, or eventually escalate to, the use of nuclear weapons.

There are an increasing number of circumstances that could precipitate the outbreak of nuclear war that neither side anticipated nor intended, possibly involving other nuclear powers or terrorist groups. There has been a relentless dispersion of the know-how, equipment and materials necessary to fabricate nuclear devices. In addition to the five declared nuclear powers, two more nations — India and Israel — are assumed to be in a position to assemble a weapon on short notice, and may already have covert stocks of nuclear devices. India, of course, has already detonated one device.

These threshold nuclear powers may be joined by at least one, and possibly two, more nations (Pakistan and South Africa) before the end of this decade. Perhaps as many as five others (Argentina, Brazil, Iraq, South Korea and Taiwan) could be in a similar position before the year 2000. Still other countries, such as Germany, Japan and Sweden, have the financial, industrial, and technological potential to fabricate nuclear weapons; they lack only the political will to do so.

At the request of Senator Nunn, General Richard Ellis, when he was commander of the Strategic Air Command, undertook an evaluation of the possibility of a third party triggering a superpower nuclear exchange under a variety of scenarios. Unfortunately, this SAC evaluation showed that there are real and developing dangers in this area.

The spread of nuclear know-how, equipment, and materials also suggests a rising danger of nuclear terrorism. While the specific risk that in any one year any particular sub-national group or rogue national leader might acquire a nuclear device is, no doubt, a low probability, the cumulative risk covering all such groups over ten or twenty years may be very great indeed. Once in the hands of such an individual or group, the potential for lawlessness would be unlimited — including extortion, revenge, or an attempt to trigger a nuclear conflict between the superpowers.

In our view, the dangers implicit in this partial catalogue of potential nuclear flashpoints indicates the necessity of the two great powers initiating discussions aimed at establishing an explicit and comprehensive system for the prevention and containment of nuclear crises.

Recent Proposals and Studies

In 1982, Senators Sam Nunn (D-Ga), John Warner (R-Va), and the late Senator Henry Jackson (D-Wa), introduced an amendment to the Defense Authorization Act requiring the Defense Department to evaluate several proposals aimed at reducing the risk of nuclear confrontations. Later that year, Senators Nunn and Warner organized the Working Group on Nuclear Risk Reduction.

In addition to the two Senators who serve as co-chairmen, the working group includes eight former civilian and military officials and technical experts. William Hyland, a senior associate at the Carnegie Endowment, serves as the group's Secretary. The other members are James Schlesinger, the former Secretary of

Defense; Brent Scowcroft, President Ford's National Security Advisor; General Richard Ellis, former Commander of the Strategic Air Command; Bobby Inman, formerly Deputy Director of Central Intelligence; William Perry, formerly Under Secretary of Defense for Research and Engineering; Don Rice, President of the Rand Corporation; and Barry Blechman, a senior fellow at the Georgetown Center for Strategic and International Studies.

In early 1983, a Defense Department study prompted by the previously mentioned legislation was released. It recommended that the existing U.S.-Soviet "Hot Line" be upgraded with a facsimile link, that an additional communications channel be installed between the Pentagon and the Soviet Defense Ministry, and that high speed communications links be established between each government and its embassy in the other's capital. These proposals were endorsed by President Reagan in May. They are now the subject of discussions between the two governments.

The proposals put forward by President Reagan are positive steps toward the development of a comprehensive system to assure the avoidance of nuclear confrontations. But there are also crucial political aspects to the problem of preventing nuclear crises. These elements can be addressed only through more comprehensive arrangements involving the designation of particular representatives and facilities in both nations that would be assigned specific responsibilities for preventing nuclear crises.

Nuclear Risk Reduction Centers

To begin, the United States and the Soviet Union might agree to establish separate national nuclear risk reduction centers in their respective capitals. These centers would maintain a 24 hour watch on any events with the potential to lead to nuclear incidents.

The nuclear risk reduction centers would have to be linked directly — both through communications channels and organizational relationships — to relevant political and military authorities. Thought might also be given to the assignment of liaison officers to the counterpart center in each capital. If this practice proved successful, it might be possible at some future time to move toward jointly manned centers in the two capitals.

An alternative arrangement would envision the creation of a single center, staffed by military and civilian representatives of the two nations, at a neutral site. Such an arrangement might facilitate closer cooperation between the U.S. and the U.S.S.R., but at the cost of diminished access between the surveillance center and the two governments themselves. This and other trade-offs between these two potential arrangements require more study.

Each center would be manned by a series of watch officers who would report through normal military and political channels. In addition, each side would designate a specific high level official to direct its center and to carry out those

specific negotiations and exchanges of information as were agreed to in establishing the centers. Procedures would be established to assure that in the event of an
emergency, the designated representatives would have direct access to each nation's highest political authority.

Direct communications links would be established between the two centers.
These should definitely include print and facsimile channels. Consideration might
also be given to the establishment of voice and perhaps even tele-conferencing
facilities, as well. There are obvious dangers in such "real-time" communications,
including the greater difficulty of intragovernmental coordination and a greater
risk of imprecision or misunderstanding, but these may be offset by the far more
rapid exchange of large amounts of information which would become possible.

The establishment of these centers could contribute significantly to a reduced
risk of nuclear incidents. They could be used for a range of functions, most of
which would take place routinely in normal times, and would be designed to
reduce the danger of nuclear terrorism, to build confidence between the two sides,
and to avoid the build-up of tensions that could lead to confrontation. It would
probably be best to define the functions of the nuclear centers narrowly at first,
expanding them as experience demonstrated the value of the enterprise.

Possible Functions of the Nuclear Risk Reduction Centers

Among the potential functions of the centers would be the following:

First, *to discuss and outline the procedures to be followed in the event of possible incidents
involving the use of nuclear weapons.* Among the contingencies that might be explored would be unexplained explosion of a nuclear device, a terrorist threat to
explode a nuclear weapon unless certain demands were met, the discovery that a
nuclear weapon was missing, and similar possibilities. The discussion of these
contingencies could provide a script which might be followed should the event
actually occur. Although neither side could be expected to commit itself to follow
these scripts under all circumstances, the existence of such an agreed routine might
facilitate appropriate actions.

Second, *to maintain close contact during incidents precipitated by nuclear terrorists,* thus
facilitating cooperative actions to defuse the incident, and specifically, to avoid the
danger that the explosion of a nuclear device by a terrorist group might lead to a
nuclear confrontation between the great powers.

Third, *to exchange information on a voluntary basis concerning events that might lead to
nuclear proliferation or to the acquisition of nuclear weapons, or the materials and equipment
necessary to build weapons, by sub-national groups.* Obviously, care would have to be
taken in any such exchange to avoid compromising intelligence sources and
methods. Still, this type of U.S.-Soviet cooperation would clearly be in their
mutual interest, and could increase both nations' ability to contain any such
threats. There have been precedents for cooperation between the two as concerns
the spread of nuclear weapons, and there is also precedent in the Standing Con-

sultative Commission established by the 1972 SALT Agreements for the confidential exchange of technical and sensitive information.

Fourth, *to exchange information about military activities which might be misunderstood by the other party during periods of mounting tensions.* At times of mounting political tensions, the existence of independent nuclear risk reduction centers might facilitate the exchange of information about military activities which might otherwise be misinterpreted and contribute to escalating suspicions and fears. Such an exchange of information would have to be made on a voluntary basis. Even so, such an exchange could help to dampen the more extreme fears and actions that could otherwise result from international conflicts. Such a system would, of course, require checks and safeguards against the possibility that disinformation would be deliberately or accidentally fed into it, leading to confusion or delays in decision-making.

Fifth, *to establish a dialogue about nuclear doctrines, forces, and activities.* These exchanges might include the notifications required under the 1971 "Accidents Agreement" and any future arrangements requiring the prior notification of missile flight tests and strategic exercises. But they could go beyond this to include discussions of any strategic practices of the two sides which implicitly raise a danger of misinterpretation or misunderstanding. Consideration also could be given to using this forum to maintain an agreed data base on the strategic forces of the two sides, a necessary element for virtually any strategic arms control agreement.

Prospects and Possibilities

A strong foundation has been laid for the proposals in this report. There have been more than 20 bilateral and multilateral treaties and agreements to which both the U.S. and U.S.S.R. are parties, that establish requirements for exchanges of information, the prior notification of certain events, the establishment of special communications links, the designation of representatives to negotiate technical aspects of the two nations' nuclear relationship, and cooperation on proliferation issues. The 1972 Incidents at Sea Agreement, which has all but eliminated what had been frequent and dangerous confrontations between the two great powers, is an excellent example of what can be accomplished.

But what already has developed on an ad hoc basis is far from comprehensive in its coverage of potential problems. Moreover, the actual use or implementation of these agreements has been limited. The current system is particularly deficient in that it does not deal adequately with the growing danger of nuclear terrorism.

We suggest that by establishing the nuclear risk reduction system described in this report, the ability of both nations to contain escalation would be greatly enhanced. The proposal deserves serious consideration by the governments of the U.S. and U.S.S.R. and by the citizens of both nations.

Appendix B
Direct Communications Links and Other Measures to Enhance Stability

Report to the Congress by Secretary of Defense Caspar W. Weinberger

To the Congress of the United States

I am pleased to submit, in accordance with Public Law 97-252, the Department of Defense evaluation of possible initiatives for improving the containment and control of nuclear weapons, particularly during crises.

I share with the Congress the conviction that we must make every effort to ensure against nuclear war ever occurring between the United States and the Soviet Union. I am equally persuaded that we can and should improve existing mechanisms to control crises which might lead to the use of nuclear weapons as a result of accident, miscalculation, or misinterpretation. Of course we should be aware that measures toward these ends, no matter how attractive at first glance, in certain cases, could entail unacceptable risks to our security and that of our allies. The Department of Defense has therefore carefully assessed the potential advantages and disadvantages of each possible new initiative intended to lower the danger of an accident or miscalculation which could lead to the use of nuclear weapons.

That evaluation has led me to propose to the President several important measures:

- The addition of a high-speed facsimile capability to the Hotline.
- The creation of a Joint Military Communications Link between the U.S. and USSR.
- The establishment by the U.S. and Soviet governments of high rate data links with their embassies in the capital of the other.
- Agreement among the world's nations to consult in the event of a nuclear incident involving a terrorist group.

Each of those measures would increase our ability to resolve crisis situations and to prevent the escalation of military incidents. Taken together, they would mark

172

significant progress toward eliminating the danger that accident or misinterpretation could lead to nuclear war.

We also have proposed for further study several possible new technical and procedural measures which might enhance our ability to verify treaty compliance and thereby further our goal of effective, significant arms control. These measures, which are outlined in the study, will be further analyzed by the Administration in the context of the development of verification measures for specific arms control treaties.

CASPAR W. WEINBERGER

I. Introduction

A. Purpose

Section 1123(a) of Public Law 97-252, dated 8 September 1982 (Department of Defense Authorization Act 1983), directs the Secretary of Defense to conduct a full and complete study and evaluation of possible initiatives for improving the containment and control of the use of nuclear weapons, particularly during crises. It also specifies that the report should address:

- Establishment of a multi-national military crisis control center for monitoring and containing the use or potential use of nuclear weapons by third parties or terrorist groups.
- Development of a forum through which the United States and the Soviet Union could exchange information pertaining to nuclear weapons that could potentially be used by third parties or terrorist groups.
- Development of other measures for building confidence between the United States and the Soviet Union in order to further crisis stability and arms control, including:

  — An improved United States–Soviet Union communications hotline for crisis control;
  — Improved procedures for verification of any arms control agreements;
  — Measures to reduce the vulnerability of command, control, and communications (C^3) systems of both nations; and
  — Measures to lengthen the warning time each nation would have of potential nuclear attack.

This report responds to that tasking. In addition, it describes ongoing U.S. initiatives already undertaken by President Reagan to reduce the risk of accidental or unintended nuclear war.

B. Agreements in Force Designed to Reduce the Risk of War

There is a long history of U.S. and Soviet efforts to reduce the threat of nuclear war between them. In fact, from the very beginning of the nuclear era, experts and government leaders expressed concern that nuclear war between the two nations could erupt unintentionally, by accident or miscalculation. As a result, various arrangements for U.S.–Soviet cooperation and consultation have been proposed and negotiated, designed to reduce the risk of misinterpretation and accidental conflict. The United States and the Soviet Union have reached agreement on several such measures.

The Memorandum of Understanding between the United States of America and the Union of Soviet Socialist Republics Regarding the Establishment of a Direct Communications Link (Hotline Agreement), signed in 1963, established a direct communications link, or Hotline, between Washington and Moscow.

The Agreement on Measures to Reduce the Risk of Outbreak of Nuclear War Between the United States of America and the Union of Soviet Socialist Republics (Accident Measures Agreement), signed in 1971, requires each side: to maintain and improve organizational and technical arrangements to guard against the accidental or unauthorized use of nuclear weapons; to notify the other side in advance of planned missile launches beyond the territory of the launching party and in the direction of the other party; and to notify the other immediately in the event of an accidental, unauthorized, or unexplained incident involving a possible detonation of a nuclear weapon which could create a risk of outbreak of nuclear war; and in the event of any unexplained nuclear incident to act in such a way as to reduce the possibility of its actions being misinterpreted by the other party.

The Agreement Between the United States of America and the Union of Soviet Socialist Republics on Measures to Improve the U.S.–USSR Direct Communications Link, signed in 1971, provided for the upgrading of the Hotline by the installation of two satellite communications circuits.

The Agreement Between the United States of America and the Union of Soviet Socialist Republics on the Prevention of Incidents on and over the High Seas (Incidents at Sea Agreement), signed in 1972, enjoins the two sides: to observe strictly the letter and the spirit of the International Regulations for Preventing Collisions at Sea; to refrain from provocative acts at sea that could increase the risk of war; and to provide advance notice to mariners of actions on the high seas which represent a danger to navigation or to aircraft in flight.

The Agreement Between the United States of America and the Union of Soviet Socialist Republics on the Prevention of Nuclear War, signed in 1973, requires that the two sides refrain from acts that could exacerbate relations between them, lead to military confrontations and/or lead to nuclear war between them or between one of them and another country. It also recognizes that each party must refrain from the threat or use of force against the other party, its allies, or other countries and to consult with the other in the event of heightened risk of nuclear war.

C. *Current Initiatives*

On 18 November 1981, President Reagan delivered the first in a series of major speeches outlining his program for preserving peace. He stated that one of the main elements of his program is to engage the Soviet Union ". . . . in a dialogue about mutual restraint and arms limitations, hoping to reduce the risk of war and the burden of armaments and to lower the barriers that divide East from West." He also took that occasion to present the general framework of his major arms control initiatives and to express his commitment to reducing the risk of surprise attack and the chance of war arising out of uncertainty or miscalculation.

President Reagan returned to this theme in his Berlin speech of 11 June 1982, and at the United Nations on 17 June 1982. He announced that we would approach the Soviet Union with proposals for reciprocal measures in such areas as advance notification of major strategic exercises, advance notification of missile launches within as well as beyond national boundaries, and an expanded exchange of strategic forces data.

On 22 November 1982, President Reagan announced to the American people that he had proposed several Confidence Building Measures (CBMs) in a letter to the Soviet leadership. He also instructed our START and INF negotiators in Geneva to discuss those proposals with their Soviet counterparts. The President's proposals reflect his belief that we must take every step possible to ensure that nuclear war cannot break out as a result of an accident, miscalculation or misunderstanding.

The measures not only include, but go beyond, the suggestions he made in Berlin and at the U.N. Thus the President proposed advance notification not only of ICBM launches but also of all launches of U.S. and Soviet submarine-launched ballistic missiles and of intermediate-range, land-based ballistic missiles of the type being negotiated in the INF talks. Additionally, he proposed an expanded exchange of data on intermediate-range nuclear forces as well as strategic forces and extended his proposal for advance notice of major strategic exercises to cover all major military exercises which might cause concern. Further, to illustrate the value of this measure, the U.S. voluntarily notified the Soviet Union in advance of its plans to begin the major military exercise named "Global Shield".

D. The "Third Party" Danger

Most of the U.S. efforts in this area have concentrated on the interaction of Soviet and U.S. forces and systems, and possible risks of nuclear war through accident, miscalculation or misunderstanding from this interaction. However, we have also paid attention to the risks that might arise from the use of nuclear weapons by a third country or subnational group.

Six nations are known to have detonated nuclear explosive devices, and a number of additional countries currently have, or could achieve, the technological and industrial capacity to develop and produce nuclear weapons. A decision to "go nuclear" could occur quickly, once a nation with the necessary technology came to regard nuclear weapons as a desirable means to respond to perceived threats, to acquire international prestige, to salvage national honor, or to compensate for loss of confidence in outside security assurances or nuclear guarantees. Compounding the problem is the possibility that a terrorist group might acquire a nuclear weapon by fabricating a crude device or by stealing one from an existing stockpile.

E. Approach of this Study

The United States and the USSR have a common interest in averting unintended or accidental nuclear war between them, and in preventing use of nuclear weapons by third nations or by terrorists that could trigger such a war. However, we must recognize that many fundamental differences between the United States and the Soviet Union complicate any effort to further that common interest through jointly agreed measures. The United States seeks to establish a stable balance of military forces and a world order based, not on the use of force, but on respect for the territorial integrity of nations. It perceives arms control measures, including CBMs, as means to help achieve these ends. While the Soviet Union professes to seek the same objectives, it encourages and takes advantage of political and military instabilities throughout the world, and is likely to exploit any ambiguities in a negotiated agreement.

The political and military interests of the United States and the Soviet Union conflict with respect to many specific nations and situations. The USSR also has a deep interest in weakening the bonds between the United States and its many friends and allies throughout the world.

Moreover, the United States and the Soviet Union differ in fundamental geographic and societal characteristics. The United States is preeminently an open society, whose government must freely share vital information about national security with the public—and thereby automatically with foreign governments. The leaders of the closed Soviet society, in contrast, maintain a heavy veil of security over their political and military activities. In addition, the Soviet Union is a large land power, contiguous to many of its allies and client states, and a short distance from many of our allies. The United States, on the other hand, is geographically distant from most of its friends and must, therefore, devote special effort to ensuring access to them.

All of those differences mean that the United States must approach prudently any effort to devise joint U.S.–Soviet measures to reduce the risk of war or to contain and control the threat of use of nuclear weapons by third countries or terrorists. In this regard, it is important not to lose sight of the fact that most of the CBMs which the USSR has proposed in the past have sought to create or to solidify Soviet geopolitical or strategic advantages. Some Soviet CBM proposals have tried to restrict our ability to come to the aid of our allies or to defend other U.S. interests. Others have aimed at ensuring Soviet conventional and/or nuclear superiority. Such proposals are, of course, unacceptable, whether they are presented on their own or as the price for Soviet agreement to measures we advocate.

We must also carefully examine any suggestions for U.S. CBM proposals to ensure that they would not inadvertently offer the Soviet Union some important unilateral benefit at our expense. We also must be alert to the possibility that any agreement could unduly restrict our ability to come to the aid of our allies, or directly harm their interests in another way. Indeed, our efforts must not only protect the interests of our allies, but must also take into account our relations with all those nations which conduct themselves in accordance with the UN Charter and other international agreements.

Finally, we must avert the possibility that the USSR could use CBMs for deception or unilateral intelligence purposes. The closed nature of Soviet society permits the Soviet government to use disinformation and deception as foreign policy tools in a way that is not acceptable—let alone feasible—for any democratic government. The fundamental purpose of CBMs could be undermined if the Soviet Union was permitted to turn them into propaganda or deception opportunities. Exceptional care must be taken to ensure that the very procedures agreed upon to reduce the risk of accidental nuclear war would not themselves become the means for the deception which would allow a premeditated surprise attack. Moreover, the United States needs to weigh carefully the possibility that measures designed to increase understanding and reduce the risk of misinterpretation could provide the Soviets with valuable, unique insights into U.S. military programs and intelligence operations, without necessarily providing the United States with comparable information or advantages.

Despite these potential drawbacks, the United States must still pursue every possible avenue to reduce the risk that war could break out between it and the Soviet Union because of accident, miscalculation, or misinterpretation. We must also try to cooperate with the USSR to limit the threat that a third party might use nuclear weapons. In so doing, however, we must be realistic about possible outcomes, approach initiatives with care, and insist that, for any new efforts undertaken, the potential benefits outweigh the risks.

II. Current Proposals to Reduce the Risk of War

The confidence building measures which the President proposed to the Soviets last November would significantly add to the range and importance of existing means to improve communication, and thus to lessen the likelihood of misinterpretation, between the United States and the Soviet Union. As the President stated in Berlin in June 1982, "Taken together, these steps would represent a qualitative improvement in the nuclear environment."

A. Notification of Ballistic Missile Launches

The President proposed to the Soviet leadership that the United States and the Soviet Union should announce in advance all launches of intercontinental ballistic missiles (ICBMs), submarine-launched ballistic missiles (SLBMs) and intermediate-range, land-based ballistic missiles of the type the U.S. and USSR are currently negotiating in Geneva. Because ballistic missiles combine high-yield warheads, accuracy, and short flight times, both sides consider them to be the most destabilizing and dangerous elements in the nuclear arsenal. Consequently, these steps to reduce the uncertainty associated with the launching of these missiles would significantly lower the risk of accidental nuclear war.

1. Intercontinental Ballistic Missile Launches

A number of previous U.S.–USSR agreements have provided for advance notification of some ICBM launches:

The 1971 "Accident Measures" Agreement requires each side to notify the other in advance of any planned missile launches which will extend beyond its national territory in the direction of the other party. Both sides have understood the Agreement to apply to land- rather than submarine-based ballistic missiles. A protocol to the Agreement requires immediate notification of an "unsuccessful" or malfunctioning launch of an unarmed missile when the trajectory of the missile extends beyond national territory in a direction that could be misinterpreted by the other side.

The 1973 Incidents at Sea agreement requires both sides to issue Notices to Airmen and Mariners (NOTAMs) for missile launches which will impact in international waters. The NOTAMs mention only the projected impact areas of the launch vehicle and associated debris. They do not specify launch point or area, the type of vehicle, or the purpose of the launch. Moreover, relatively few Soviet launches are covered by the agreement, whereas virtually all U.S. ICBM and SLBM launches are directed to the open ocean.

The SALT II Treaty would have obligated each party to notify the other well in advance of any multiple ICBM launches or of single ICBM launches which would extend beyond its national territory. Unlike the NOTAMs required under the Incidents at Sea Agreement, the SALT notifications we sought would have included detailed information (e.g., launch locations, test range) and would have been provided directly to the other side. The U.S. began providing notifications in July 1979, consistent with its desire that the two countries act in accord with appropriate provisions of the SALT II Treaty even though it was not ratified. The Soviets also have provided notifications, albeit not as detailed as the U.S. notifications.

None of the previous agreements provides total coverage of all ICBM launches. In particular, they do not cover single launches which impact within the territory of the launching nation. Because any launch can create some uncertainty and ambiguity, the U.S. has proposed in the START negotiations that the sides provide notice of all ICBM launches, whether they occur singly or in multiples, whether their flights remain within national boundaries or extend beyond them. This proposal would carry the additional benefits of equalizing the current obligations on each side for advance notification and of discouraging the use of missile launches for geopolitical purposes such as a "show-of-force."

2. Submarine-Launched Ballistic Missile Launches

The United States and the USSR do not now notify each other directly or specifically of SLBM launches. They only issue standard NOTAMs which announce air space and ocean "closure areas" if they expect an SLBM to impact in international waters. They do not, however, specify the reason for the closures. The President has, therefore, proposed that the two sides provide specific advance notification of all SLBM launches, including any which impact within national territory. This, combined with the ICBM notification proposal, would mean that for the first time, advance notice would be required for all launches of strategic ballistic missiles in the arsenals of either side.

3. LRINF Ballistic Missile Launches

Finally, the United States has proposed that both sides provide advance notification of all launches of land-based longer-range intermediate-range nuclear force (LRINF) ballistic missiles. These include the Soviet Union's SS-20, SS-4, and SS-5 missiles, and the U.S. Pershing II. We continue to seek the elimination of all land-based American and Soviet LRINF missiles. While we are negotiating that ban, however, we believe that notification of all LRINF ballistic missile launches would have some net benefits.

III. Possible New Measures to Enhance Communication

One of the most effective ways to further the effort already begun by President Reagan to ensure against unintended nuclear conflict between the United States and the Soviet Union would be to improve the ability of the two to communicate about crises and military incidents. In examining possible new initiatives for reducing the threat of nuclear weapons use, the Department of Defense has therefore focused on ways of increasing the speed, reliability, accuracy, and completeness of direct communication between the United States and the Soviet Union. In addition, we have studied whether improved communications with other countries could lower the risk of war.

A. Hotline Improvements

A priority measure to enhance communications is to improve the Direct Communications Link (DCL, or "Hotline") between the U.S. and Soviet heads of government. The Hotline is, and should remain, for use only in severe emergencies. It would degrade the system, and reduce its impact in major crises, if it were used in cases that could be handled effectively through routine or lower-level bilateral channels.

In keeping with the Hotline mission, the precise number of times that the two heads of state have used it has not been disclosed. It is known that it has been used sparingly during its twenty-year existence, but it has proved invaluable in major crises. U.S. Presidents have cited its use during the 1967 Arab-Israeli War to prevent possible Soviet misunderstanding of U.S. fleet movements in the Mediterranean and during the 1973 Arab-Israeli War.

The United States and the Soviet Union have significantly upgraded the DCL once since its creation. The system originally consisted of two terminal points with teletype equipment, one full-time duplex wire telegraph circuit (routed Washington-London-Copenhagen-Stockholm-Helsinki-Moscow), and for back-up, one full-time duplex radio-telegraph circuit (routed Washington-Tangier-Moscow). In 1971, the two governments agreed to establish two satellite communication circuits for the DCL, with a system of multiple terminals in each country. When those became operational in 1978, the DCL achieved almost 100 percent technical reliability. The original radio circuit was terminated, while the wire telegraph circuit remains as a back-up.

1. Facsimile Transmission Capability

The Department of Defense has now proposed for consideration by the President the addition of a high-speed facsimile capability to the system. This improvement would increase the DCL's ability for conveying information by enabling the two sides to transmit more, and more complex, data more quickly and reliably. The time saved—even though limited by the slowness of the translation process—could be used to send more messages or for increased deliberation and consultation on each side. In addition, a facsimile transmission capability would minimize or entirely eliminate the need for keyboarding, and therefore the possibility of operator error.

Most important, facsimile equipment would endow the Hotline with a capability which it does not now possess: the ability to exchange graphic information. The precise, detailed, and often easily interpreted information offered by maps, charts, and drawings could be essential in resolving an on-going military crisis. Because graphic information requires little or no translation, the total time saved through this improvement could actually be much greater than that implied simply by the increase in the transmission rate. Translation is the slowest step in the direct communication process. A highly proficient Russian language specialist can produce a full translation at the rate of only 1,000 words per hour, and do a cursory review at the rate of 6,000 words per hour.

2. Voice and Video Capability

The Department of Defense has also considered the possibility of adding a secure voice or video capability to the DCL. We have concluded, however, that this step would carry many more disadvantages than advantages. The United States and the Soviet Union explicitly decided not to include voice capability when they negotiated the original Hotline agreement and its subsequent improvement. On both occasions, they concluded that printed communication would be more private, more precise, and more reliable. The studies leading to this report reinforce that conclusion.

Because voice communication is more difficult than written material to translate, it is far more subject to misunderstanding. In addition, a direct conversation could encourage instant response, thereby denying the head of state the necessary opportunity to consult with advisors and prepare a thoughtful and measured response. For both reasons, emergency voice communications between the two leaders could reduce, rather than heighten, their ability to resolve a crisis. The same considerations apply, in heightened fashion, to the installation of video conferencing capability.

B. *Possible New Communications Mechanisms*

1. Bilateral Joint Military Communications Link

One measure which we are now considering would create a Joint Military Communications Link (JMCL), paralleling the DCL, between the United States and the Soviet Union. A JMCL would provide a direct facsimile transmission capability between the two national crisis control centers (in the United States, the National Military Command Center in the Pentagon). It would supplement, but not supplant, existing diplomatic channels.

Placing a JMCL in the national military command centers would enable us to build on and strengthen the existing rapid communications system, and reduce requirements for additional personnel, training, etc. Also, it would allow rapid exchange of highly technical information that could be essential to understanding and therefore resolving a nuclear or other military crisis. No existing communication channel between the United States and the USSR has a similar capability.

A JMCL could be used to implement agreements on the sharing of military information that is time urgent. It could, for example, be the mechanism for the consultations on terrorist nuclear activity that we discuss later in this report. It could also be the designated vehicle for the ballistic missile launch and military exercise notifications proposed by the President.

A JMCL could also have a crisis control function. It could be used in the event of any military incident that required urgent communication between the United States and the USSR, but did not warrant direct contact between the two heads of government.

A JMCL could also be used for cooperation—rather than avoidance of confrontation—between the two countries in certain urgent situations. For example, if a military craft of the one side were lost or disabled, a JMCL would facilitate assistance by the other. Similarly, it could ensure proper handling of any space objects with nuclear components which threatened to impact on land.

We believe that exercises of a JMCL and its regular use for implementing information-sharing agreements would go far toward ensuring that the system would work well in any crisis. The information-sharing function of a JMCL would provide both sides with a series of opportunities—in time-sensitive, but not emergency, situations—to increase their familiarity with the system and to identify any procedural changes which would heighten its usefulness in a military crisis.

Joint U.S.–Soviet exercises of a JCML could also offer an important vehicle for refining and building each side's confidence in the system.

2. Multilateral Military Communications Link

While the bilateral JMCL concept could enhance communication and reduce the risk of war arising from miscalculation or misinterpretation, we believe that a multilateral MCL would not be desirable. It would be extremely difficult to determine which states to include in a multilateral network. The addition of too many states would threaten to make a MCL so unwieldy that it would never function effectively.

3. Embassy-Capital High Rate Data Communication Link

Another promising method of improving crisis communications between the United States and the Soviet Union could be for each to establish high rate data links between its head of government and its embassy in the other's capital. We believe that such a system could provide an important supplement to the DCL and to a JMCL.

Each government would install and control its own system, using its own technology. Nevertheless, introduction of the system would require consent pursuant to the 1961 Vienna Convention on Diplomatic Privileges and Immunities. A bilateral agreement would also be essential to ensure that each government agreed to allow the other to bring in the necessary equipment freely and without interference.

4. Crisis Control Center

We have also carefully considered the suggestions for a U.S.–Soviet or multinational crisis control center, but have concluded that it would not be desirable to establish such an institution at this time. Over time, our experience with operating a JMCL might allow us to pursue the idea of a crisis control center, by indicating ways in which we could reduce the risks involved in it to an acceptable level. We doubt, however, that a multilateral crisis control center located in a neutral country will ever be feasible. We expect that the use of a JMCL would be more likely to point the way to a bilateral mechanism linking separate crisis control bodies located in Washington and Moscow.

A crisis control center located in a neutral country would be far removed from the national capitals where crisis decisions would have to be made. This separation would present several serious drawbacks. It is most likely that a center would be completely bypassed in national crisis decisionmaking. If not, a center would create a cumbersome extra layer in the national and international decision processes, retarding action just when speed was most imperative. Moreover, flexibility in deciding when to communicate, which would be an important feature of a JMCL, would be difficult to achieve in an institutionalized U.S.–Soviet crisis control center. The institution would provide a clear and legitimate channel for automatic consideration of any crisis—including those in which Soviet participation would serve to heighten, rather than reduce, tensions.

A multilateral crisis control center would suffer from even more problems. The more members in a center, the less likely that they would all share a common interest in preventing the outbreak or escalation of conflict. Even if that were not the case, the decisionmaking process in a multinational center would easily become bogged down, and inhibit timely, concerted actions to avert a serious crisis. Indeed, there would be a general risk that the facility would evolve from a confidential tool for crisis management into a forum for waging propaganda warfare over sensitive crises.

Finally, the expansion of the number of recipients of shared information would increase the danger that a member government might use the facility to spread disinformation or misuse gathered information. With unrestricted membership, it would be impossible by definition to exchange intelligence data. Any shared information would immediately be in the public domain.

5. Information Sharing Facility

A U.S.–Soviet institution for sharing information on nuclear activities by third countries or terrorists would present many of the problems associated with a crisis control center and add new ones. Since such a body would concentrate on information exchange, the risks would increase that the Soviets could transform it into a new source of sensitive intelligence data or attempt to exploit it for disinformation purposes. Those risks would be compounded if an effort was made to endow the institution with a general data bank or if it was made a multilateral rather than bilateral forum.

Although an information-sharing institution therefore does not seem feasible, we are considering a multilateral agreement providing for consultations during particular nuclear crises. Nations party to the agreement would, when they deemed appropriate, consult with each other on nuclear explosions or acquisition of nuclear weapons by terrorist groups. By limiting the consultation to an aspect of the nuclear proliferation problem that is of particular concern to virtually all states, the agreement would minimize the risk that a nation would use it for disinformation purposes.

IV. Additional Measures to Reduce Ambiguity and Misinterpretation

In addition to the enhanced communication mechanisms discussed in the previous section, the Department of Defense has considered a number of other measures which might reduce ambiguity surrounding military incidents, and thus lessen the possibility of misinterpretation. These fall into three general categories: improved arms control verification procedures; improved warning of nuclear attack; and reduced vulnerability of command, control, and communication systems.

A. *Enchanced Verification Procedures for Nuclear Arms Control Agreements*

Effective verification is essential to effective arms control. The first requirement for effective verification is possession of satisfactory monitoring capability. Towards this end, the United States maintains an extensive intelligence capability for monitoring treaty-limited activities and invests heavily in new technologies which may improve our ability to monitor activity related to treaty compliance.

Effective verification depends on satisfying a series of non-technical conditions as well. Our verification efforts cannot rely solely on intelligence community monitoring of the other side to evade detection, and our own ability to counter cheating. We must assess the incentive of the other side to cheat. We must also assess the political and military significance of potential violations, recognizing that charges of treaty violation are not easily made nor easily accepted, especially when evidence based upon the most sensitive intelligence sources and methods is involved. Enforcement of compliance under these circumstances is even more difficult.

The verification provisions of U.S.–USSR arms control treaties vary widely. Some agreements, such as the Biological Weapons Convention, do not include express verifications measures, but instead simply provide for consultations about compliance. Other agreements, like the SALT I Interim Agreement and the ABM Treaty explicit refer to national technical means of verification (NTM), and provide supplements to NTM through counting rules and collateral measures such as dismantlement and destruction procedures. The SALT II verification provisions appeared to go further by including telemetry encryption under measures that could be defined as deliberate concealment measures. In fact, however, some SALT II provisions were ambiguous and provided an inadequate basis for judging compliance.

The information needed by the West for effective verification of arms control agreements generally requires disclosure of what the Soviet Union considers to be state secrets—even though it may involve information normally made public in the West. Consequently, except for such collateral measures as dismantlement and destruction procedures, the Soviet Union typically prefers caveated or ambiguous wording which makes it difficult to challenge its compliance with verification rules.

The Soviet Union's callous disregard of the 1972 Biological Weapons Convention by producing deadly toxins and of the 1925 Geneva Protocol by using and encouraging the use of deadly toxins against combatants and innocent civilians in Southeast Asia provides the most compelling explanation of why, in the future, the U.S. must insist that arms control agreements with the USSR contain effective verification provisions.

We have examined several technical and procedural measures which could enhance verification capabilities and thereby contribute to mutual confidence between the United States and the Soviet Union. These include the use of combined consultative commissions, international verification bodies, data exchanges and other measures beyond National Technical Means of verification. All, however, require further analysis in the context of specific treaty requirements.

B. *Measures to Lengthen Warning Time of Potential Attack*

Many of the initiatives discussed earlier in this report—the President's proposals for ballistic missile launch notifications, the Joint Military Communications Link, the high rate data link between each side's capital and its embassy in the other country, the agreement to consult during crises involving terrorist nuclear activity—would heighten U.S. and Soviet awareness of—and thereby ability to divert—any near-term danger of a nuclear accident or attack. We have also examined more technical measures which might enhance U.S. and Soviet warning capabilities, whether the threat comes from the other party, from a third country, or from a terrorist or subnational group. After careful study, however, we have concluded that none of the possible bilateral U.S.–Soviet measures available for increasing warning time would have enough utility to warrant its continued consideration.

C. *Measures to Reduce Vulnerability of Command, Control and Communications (C³) on Both Sides*

Finally, we have examined possible bilateral U.S.–Soviet and unilateral approaches to reduce the vulnerability of our command, control and communications (C^3) systems—the systems necessary to communicate with and direct strategic forces.

The strategic C^3 system is vital to ensure that strategic forces can respond to attack, and is therefore an essential element of deterrence. The system also guarantees that the ultimate control over nuclear weapons resides at the highest national decision-making level. The C^3 system provides the essential intermediary between our nuclear attack warning system and the decision-makers who would determine a response to a nuclear attack. Thus, it must be capable of performing its functions both during and after attacks.

Shortly after President Reagan took office in 1981, he directed that a thorough review be conducted of the strategic C^3 system and its ability to function under and survive attack. When the President announced his Strategic Modernization Program, he gave the highest priority to correcting strategic deficiencies. Major initiatives for achieving these C^3 corrections are now under way. President Reagan's decision was made in response to ten years of neglect of U.S. C^3 capability and survivability, as well as a sustained Soviet C^3 improvement program. That Soviet effort has not only strengthened the Soviet strategic C^3 system but also increased its ability to target and destroy U.S. strategic forces and associated C^3.

The modernization program for strategic C^3 calls for balanced improvements in essential capabilities, including upgrading of the survivability and endurance of the alert warning and attack assessment sensors, increasing mobility and endurance of command decision-making functions, extensively improving communications, and assuring means for recovery and reconstitution of U.S. strategic forces following a major nuclear attack.

Appendix C
Text of the 1963 Hot Line Agreement with 1971 and 1984 Amendments

MEMORANDUM OF UNDERSTANDING BETWEEN THE UNITED STATES OF AMERICA AND THE UNION OF SOVIET SOCIALIST REPUBLICS REGARDING THE ESTABLISHMENT OF A DIRECT COMMUNICATIONS LINK

Signed at Geneva June 20, 1963
Entered into force June 20, 1963

For use in time of emergency the Government of the United States of America and the Government of the Union of Soviet Socialist Republics have agreed to establish as soon as technically feasible a direct communications link between the two Governments.

Each Government shall be responsible for the arrangements for the link on its own territory. Each Government shall take the necessary steps to ensure continuous functioning of the link and prompt delivery to its head of government of any communications received by means of the link from the head of government of the other party.

Arrangements for establishing and operating the link are set forth in the Annex which is attached hereto and forms an integral part hereof.

DONE in duplicate in the English and Russian languages at Geneva, Switzerland, this 20th day of June, 1963.

Acting Representative of the United States of America to the Eighteen-Nation Committee on Disarmament

Acting Representative of the Soviet Socialist Republics to the Eighteen-Nation Committee on Disarmament

ANNEX

TO THE MEMORANDUM OF UNDERSTANDING BETWEEN THE
UNITED STATES OF AMERICA AND THE UNION OF SOVIET
SOCIALIST REPUBLICS REGARDING THE ESTABISHMENT OF A
DIRECT COMMUNICATIONS LINK

The direct communications link between Washington and Moscow established in
accordance with the Memorandum, and the operation of such link, shall be
governed by the following provisions:

1. The direct communications link shall consist of:

   a. Two terminal points with telegraph-teleprinter equipment between
      which communications shall be directly exchanged;
   b. One full-time duplex wire telegraph circuit, routed Washington-
      London-Copenhagen-Stockholm-Helsinki-Moscow, which shall be
      used for the transmission of messages;
   c. One full-time duplex radiotelegraph circuit, routed Washington-
      Tangier-Moscow, which shall be used for service communications and
      for coordination of operations between the two terminal points.

If experience in operating the direct communications link should demonstrate
that the establishment of an additional wire telegraph circuit is advisable, such
circuit may be established by mutual agreement between authorized representatives of both Governments.

2. In case of interruption of the wire circuit, transmission of messages shall be
effected via the radio circuit, and for this purpose provision shall be made at the
terminal points for the capability of prompt switching of all necessary equipment
from one circuit to another.

3. The terminal points of the link shall be so equipped as to provide for the
transmission and reception of messages from Moscow to Washington in the
Russian language and from Washington to Moscow in the English language. In
this connection the USSR shall furnish the United States four sets of telegraph
terminal equipment, including page printers, transmitters, and reperforators, with
one year's supply of spare parts and all necessary special tools, test equipment,
operating instructions, and other technical literature, to provide for transmission
and reception of messages in the Russian language.

The United States shall furnish the Soviet Union four sets of telegraph terminal
equipment, including page printers, transmitters, and reperforators, with one
year's supply of spare parts and all necessary special tools, test equipment, operating instructions and other technical literature, to provide for transmission and
reception of messages in the English language.

The equipment described in this paragraph shall be exchanged directly between
the parties without any payment being required therefor.

4.　The terminal points of the direct communications link shall be provided with encoding equipment. For the terminal point in the USSR, four sets of such equipment (each capable of simplex operation), with one year's supply of spare parts, with all necessary special tools, test equipment, operating instructions and other technical literature, and with all necessary blank tape, shall be furnished by the United States to the USSR against payment of the cost thereof by the USSR.

The USSR shall provide for preparation and delivery of keying tapes to the terminal point of the link in the United States for reception of messages from the USSR. The United States shall provide for the preparation and delivery of keying tapes to the terminal point of the link in the USSR for reception of messages from the United States. Delivery of prepared keying tapes to the terminal points of the link shall be effected through the Embassy of the USSR in Washington (for the terminal of the link in the USSR) and through the Embassy of the United States in Moscow (for the terminal of the link in the United States).

5.　The United States and the USSR shall designate the agencies responsible for the arrangements regarding the direct communications link, for its technical maintenance, continuity and reliability, and for the timely transmission of messages.

Such agencies may, by mutual agreement, decide matters and develop instructions relating to the technical maintenance and operation of the direct communications link and effect arrangements to improve the operation of the link.

6.　The technical parameters of the telegraph circuits of the link and of the terminal equipment, as well as the maintenance of such circuits and equipment, shall be in accordance with CCITT and CCIR recommendations.

Transmission and reception of messages over the direct communications link shall be effected in accordance with applicable recommendations of international telegraph and radio communications regulations, as well as with mutually agreed instructions.

7.　The costs of the direct communications link shall be borne as follows:

a.　The USSR shall pay the full cost of leasing the portion of the telegraph circuit from Moscow to Helsinki and 50% of the cost of leasing the portion of the telegraph circuit from Helsinki to London. The United States shall pay the full cost of leasing the portion of the telegraph circuit from Washington to London and 50% of the cost of leasing the portion of the telegraph circuit from London to Helsinki.

b.　Payment of the cost of leasing the radio telegraph circuit between Washington and Moscow shall be effected without any transfer of payments between the parties. The USSR shall bear the expenses relating to the transmission of messages from Moscow to Washington. The United States shall bear the expenses relating to the transmission of messages from Washington to Moscow.

Agreement between the United States of America and the Union of Soviet Socialist Republics on Measures to Improve the USA-USSR Direct Communications Link

Signed at Washington September 30, 1971
Entered into force September 30, 1971

The United States of America and the Union of Soviet Socialist Republics, hereinafter referred to as the Parties.

Noting the positive experience gained in the process of operating the existing Direct Communications Link between the United States of America and the Union of Soviet Socialist Republics, which was established for use in time of emergency pursuant to the Memorandum of Understanding Regarding the Establishment of a Direct Communications Link, signed on June 20, 1963,

Having examined, in a spirit of mutual understanding, matters relating to the improvement and modernization of the Direct Communications Link,

Having agreed as follows:

Article 1

1. For the purpose of increasing the reliability of the Direct Communications Link, there shall be established and put into operation the following:

   (a.) two additional circuits between the United States of America and the Union of Soviet Socialist Republics each using a satellite communications system, with each party selecting a satellite communications system of its own choice.

   (b.) a system of terminals (more than one) in the territory of each party for the Direct Communications Link, with the locations and number of terminals in the United States of America to be determined by the United States side, and the locations and number of terminals in the Union of Soviet Socialist Republics to be determined by the Soviet side.

2. Matters relating to the implementation of the aforementioned improvements of the Direct Communications Link are set forth in the Annex which is attached hereto and forms an integral part hereof.

Article 2

Each Party confirms its intention to take all possible measures to assure the continuous and reliable operation of the communications circuits and the system of terminals of the Direct Communications Link for which it is responsible in accordance with this Agreement and the Annex hereto, as well as to communicate to the head of its Government any messages received via the Direct Communications Link from the head of Government of the other party.

Article 3

The Memorandum of Understanding Between the United States of America and the Union of Soviet Socialist Republics Regarding the Establishment of a Direct Communications Link, signed on June 20, 1963, with the Annex thereto, shall remain in force, except to the extent that its provisions are modified by this Agreement and Annex hereto.

Article 4

The undertakings of the parties hereunder shall be carried out in accordance with their respective Constitutional processes.

Article 5

This Agreement, including the Annex hereto, shall enter into force upon signature.

DONE at Washington on September 30, 1971, in two copies, each in the English and Russian languages, both texts being equally authentic.

FOR THE UNITED STATES   FOR THE UNION OF SOVIET
OF AMERICA   SOCIALIST REPUBLICS:

UNITED STATES AND SOVIET NOTES ON UPGRADE OF THE
DIRECT COMMUNICATIONS LINK—JULY 17, 1984

United States Note

The Department of State, referring to the Memorandum of Understanding between the United States of America and the Union of Soviet Socialist Republics regarding the Establishment of a Direct Communications Link, signed June 20, 1963; to the Agreement on Measures to Improve the Direct Communications Link, signed September 30, 1971; and to the exchange of views between the two parties in Moscow and Washington during which it was deemed desirable to arrange for facsimile communication in addition to the current teletype Direct Communications Link, proposes that for this purpose the parties shall:

1. Establish and maintain three transmission links employing INTELSAT and STATSIONAR satellites and cable technology with secure orderwire circuit for operational monitoring. In this regard:

(a) Each party shall provide communications circuits capable of simultaneously transmitting and receiving 4800 bits per second.

(b) Operation of facsimile communication shall begin with the test operation over the INTELSAT satellite channel as soon as development, procurement and delivery of the necessary equipment by the sides are completed.

(c) Facsimile communication via STATSIONAR shall be established after transition of the Direct Communications Link teletype circuit from MOLNIYA to STATSIONAR using mutually agreeable transition procedures and after successful tests of facsimile communication via INTELSAT and cable.

2. Employ agreed-upon information security devices to assure secure transmission of facsimile materials. In this regard:

(a) The information security devices shall consist of microprocessors that will combine the digital facsimile output with buffered random data read from standard 5¼ inch floppy disks. The American side shall provide a specification describing the key data format and necessary keying material resident on a floppy disk for both parties until such time as the Soviet side develops this capability. Beyond that time, each party shall provide necessary keying material to the other.

(b) The American side shall provide to the Soviet side the floppy disk drives integral to the operation of the microprocessor.

(c) The necessary security devices as well as spare parts for the said equipment shall be provided by the American side to the Soviet side in return for payment of costs thereof by the Soviet side.

3. Establish and maintain at each operating end of the Direct Communications Link facsimile terminals of the same make and model. In this regard:

(a) Each party shall be responsible for the acquisition, installation, operation and maintenance of its own facsimile machines, the related information security devices, and local transmission circuits appropriate to the implementation of this understanding, except as otherwise specified.

(b) A Group III facsimile unit which meets CCITT Recommendations T.4 and T.30 and operates at 4800 bits per second shall be used for this purpose.

(c) The necessary facsimile equipment as well as spare parts for the said equipment shall be provided to the Soviet side by the American side in return for payment of costs thereof by the Soviet side.

4. Establish and maintain secure orderwire communications necessary for coordination of facsimile operation. In this regard:

(a) The orderwire terminals used with the information security devices described in Paragraph 2(a) shall incorporate standard U.S.S.R. Cyrillic and United States Latin keyboards and cathode ray tube displays to permit telegraphic exchange of information between operators. The specific layout of the Cyrillic keyboard shall be as specified by the Soviet side.

(b) To coordinate the work of the facsimile equipment operators, an orderwire shall be configured so as to permit, prior to the transmission and reception of facsimile messages, the exchange of all information pertinent to the coordination of such messages.

(c) Orderwire messages concerning facsimile transmissions shall be encoded using the same information security devices specified in Paragraph 2(a).

(d) The orderwire shall use the same modem and communications link as used for facsimile transmission.

(e) A printer shall be included to provide a record copy of all information exchanged on the orderwire.

(f) The necessary orderwire equipment as well as spare parts for the said equipment shall be provided by the American side to the Soviet side, in return for payment of costs thereof by the Soviet side.

5. Ensure the exchange of information necessary for the operation and maintenance of the facsimile system.

6. Take all possible measures to assure the continuous, secure and reliable operation of the facsimile equipment, information security devices and communications links including orderwire, for which each party is responsible in accordance with this agreement.

The Department of State also proposes that the parties, in consideration of the continuing advances in information and communications technology, conduct reviews as necessary regarding questions concerning improvement of the Direct Communications Link and its technical maintenance.

It is also proposed to note that the Memorandum of Understanding between the United States of America and the Union of Soviet Socialist Republic regarding the Establishment of a Direct Communications Link, signed on June 20, 1963, with the Annex thereto; the Agreement between the United States of America and the Union of the Soviet Socialist Republics on Measures to Improve the Direct Communications Link, with the Annex thereto, signed on September 30, 1971; those Understandings, with Attached Annexes, reached between the United States and Union of Soviet Socialist Republics delegations of technical specialists and experts signed on September 11, 1972, December 10, 1973, March 22, 1976, and the exchange of notes at Moscow on March 20 and April 29, 1975, constituting an Agreement Amending the Agreement of September 30, 1971, remain in force, except to the extent that their provisions are modified by this agreement.

If the foregoing is acceptable to the Soviet side, it is proposed that this note, together with the reply of the Embassy of the Union of Soviet Socialist Republics, shall constitute an agreement, effective on the date of the Embassy's reply.

Soviet Reply

The Embassy of the Union of Soviet Socialist Republics acknowledges the receipt of the Department of State's Note of July 17, 1984, which reads as follows:

(Quotation of entire text of U.S. note)

The Embassy of the U.S.S.R. states that the Soviet side agrees to the proposals contained in the note of the Department of State. Therefore, that note, together with this reply, shall constitute an agreement, effective on the date of the Embassy's reply.

Appendix D
Text of the 1971 "Accidents Treaty"

AGREEMENT ON MEASURES TO REDUCE THE RISK OF
OUTBREAK OF NUCLEAR WAR BETWEEN THE UNITED STATES
OF AMERICA AND THE UNION OF SOVIET SOCIALIST
REPUBLICS

Signed at Washington September 30, 1971
Entered in force September 30, 1971

The United States of America and the Union of Soviet Socialist Republics, hereinafter referred to as the parties:

Taking into account the devastating consequences that nuclear war would have for all mankind, and recognizing the need to exert every effort to avert the risk of outbreak of such a war, including measures to guard against accidental or un-authorized use of nuclear weapons,

Believing that agreement on measures for reducing the risk of outbreak of nuclear war serves the interests of strengthening international peace and security, and is in no way contrary to the interests of any other country,

Bearing in mind that continued efforts are also needed in the future to seek ways of reducing the risk of outbreak of nuclear war,

Have agreed as follows:

Article 1
Each Party undertakes to maintain and to improve, as it deems necessary, its existing organizational and technical arrangements to guard against the accidental or unauthorized use of nuclear weapons under its control.

Article 2

The Parties undertake to notify each other immediately in the event of an accidental, unauthorized or any other unexplained incident involving a possible detonation of a nuclear weapon which could create a risk of outbreak of nuclear war. In the event of such an incident, the party whose nuclear weapon is involved will immediately make every effort to take necessary measures to render harmless or destroy such weapon without its causing damage.

Article 3

The Parties undertake to notify each other immediately in the event of detection by missile warning systems of unidentified objects, or in the event of signs of interference with these systems or with related communications facilities, if such occurrences could create a risk of outbreak of nuclear war between the two countries.

Article 4

Each Party undertakes to notify the other party in advance of any planned missile launches if such launches will extend beyond its national territory in the direction of the other Party.

Article 5

Each Party, in other situations involving unexplained nuclear incidents, undertakes to act in such a manner as to reduce the possibility of its actions being misinterpreted by the other Party. In any such situation, each Party may inform the other Party or request information when, in its view, this is warranted by the interests of averting the risk of outbreak of nuclear war.

Article 6

For transmission of urgent information, notifications and requests for information in situations requiring prompt clarification, the parties shall make primary use of the Direct Communications Link between the Governments of the United States of America and the Union of Soviet Socialist Republics.

For transmission of other information, notifications and requests for information, the parties, at their own discretion, may use any communications facilities, including diplomatic channels, depending on the degree of urgency.

Article 7

The Parties undertake to hold consultations, as mutually agreed, to consider questions relating to implementation of the provisions of this Agreement, as well as to discuss possible amendments thereto aimed at further implementation of the purposes of this Agreement.

Article 8
This Agreement shall be of unlimited duration.

Article 9
This Agreement shall enter into force upon signature.

DONE at Washington on September 30, 1971, in two copies, each in the English and Russian languages, both texts being equally authentic.

FOR THE UNITED STATES
OF AMERICA:

FOR THE UNION OF SOVIET
SOCIALIST REPUBLICS:

CONTRIBUTORS

Barry M. Blechman is president of Defense Forecasts, Inc., and a senior fellow at Georgetown University's Center for Strategic and International Studies. He has published widely on issues of foreign and defense policies.

Richard K. Betts is a senior fellow at the Brookings Institution and the author of *Soldiers, Statesmen, and Cold War-Crises* and *Surprise Attack* and coauthor of *The Irony of Vietnam*.

Sidney D. Drell is professor, deputy director, and executive head of theoretical physics of Stanford Linear Accelerator Center, Stanford University, and co-director of the Stanford Center for International Security and Arms Control.

William J. Lynn is a research associate at Georgetown University's Center for Strategic and International Studies and executive director of the CSIS Defense Organization Project.

Senator Sam Nunn is the ranking Democrat on the Senate Armed Services Committee. He also serves on the Intelligence Committee, the Small Business Committee and the Government Affairs Committee.

Joseph S. Nye, Jr., is Dillon Professor of International Affairs at Harvard University. His most recent book (coauthored) is *Living with Nuclear Weapons* (1983).

Theodore J. Ralston is director of the International Liaison Office, Micro-Electronic Computer Corporation, and a member of the Center for International Security and Arms Control, Stanford University.

James A. Thomson directs Rand's Research Programs on National Strategy. He was previously a member of the National Security Council Staff and worked in the Office of the Secretary of Defense.

Victor A. Utgoff is deputy director of Strategy Forces and Resources Division at the Institute for Defense Analyses. He was previously director of Policy Analysis with the National Security Council Staff.

Alan J. Vick is a staff member with the Rand Corporation, specializing in strategic issues. He received his Ph.D. from the University of California, Irvine.

Senator John Warner has served as secretary of the navy, in which capacity he negotiated the Incidents at Sea Treaty. He is currently the third ranking Republican on the Senate Armed Services Committee and chairman of its Subcommittee on Strategic and Nuclear Forces.

Colonel Wade J. Williams, U.S. Army, is a career military intelligence officer. He is currently assigned to the Policy and Plans Directorate (J-5) of the Joint Chiefs of Staff.